Independent
Coffee Guide
North, Midlands
& North Wales
is supported by

ATKINSONS
COFFEE ROASTERS

FOR BREW FREAKS, BEAN GEEKS

AND THE SIMPLY CURIOUS ...

- THE BEST COFFEE DESERVES -
THE NATION'S No.1
ORGANIC MILK*

By supporting Yeo Valley Organic Milk, you're helping us build more vital hives for British bees on our organic dairy farms.

*Source: Kantar FMCG, Total Market, Total Organic Dairy, 52 w/e 5th September 2021

We are organic right down to our roots, meaning the soil on our farms is full of life and the fields and hedgerows are naturally buzzing with wildlife.

Did you know organic farmers don't use damaging chemical pesticides and artificial fertilisers? This means our land is a safe and flourishing habitat for all the little creatures above and below the ground.

- Our 100% organic milk is sourced from organic British dairy farms

- Delivering great tasting consistent quality

- Perfect for a full flavoured coffee

- Sourced from organic free-range cows

VISIT ARLAPRO.COM FOR MORE INFORMATION

Independent Coffee Guide **team:**

Richard Bailey, Nick Cooper,
Andy Greeves, Kathryn Lewis, Abi Manning,
Melissa Morris, Christopher Mulholland,
Amy Pay, Tamsin Powell, Jo Rees, Rosanna
Rothery, Mark Tibbles and Selena Young.

A big thank you to the *Independent Coffee
Guide* **committee** (meet them on page 206)
for their expertise and enthusiasm, and to our
headline sponsor Yeo Valley and **sponsors**
Arla, Atkinsons, Blue Diamond, Cakesmiths,
Cup North, Independent Coffee Box, Kokoa
Collection and VA Machinery.

Coffee shops, cafes and roasteries are invited
to be included in the guide based on meeting
criteria set by the committee, which includes
the use of speciality beans, providing a high-
quality coffee experience for visitors and being
independently run.

For information on *Independent Coffee Guides*
for Ireland, Scotland, and South England and
South Wales, visit:

www.indycoffee.guide

 @indycoffeeguide

© Salt Media Ltd
Published by Salt Media Ltd 2021
www.saltmedia.co.uk
01271 859299
ideas@saltmedia.co.uk

Contents

Page

14   Welcome

16   How to use the guide

18   Your adventures start here

20   Northumberland, Tyne and Wear & County Durham

34   Cumbria, Lancashire & Merseyside

70   North Wales

84   Greater Manchester & Cheshire

116   Yorkshire

166   The Midlands

200   More good coffee shops

204   More good roasteries

208   Meet our committee

212   Index

Welcome

The world has changed beyond belief since we published the previous *North, Midlands & North Wales Independent Coffee Guide* in November 2019, yet the community spirit of the UK speciality coffee scene remains as vibrant as ever.

There have, of course, been some casualties as a result of the lockdowns. However, it's inspiring to see so many coffee shops and roasteries bounce back stronger thanks to the dedication of the loyal customers who've supported them through the pandemic.

Despite the testing times, you'll find lots of new venues in this updated edition. From Newcastle to Wakefield, Llangollen to Nottingham, a whole host of fresh speciality venues have sprung up that are definitely worth adding to your coffee hit-list.

Roasteries have been shaking things up too, and many have opened on-site espresso bars and introduced roastery tours. So, as you travel these caffeine-rich regions, don't miss the opportunity to visit them to breathe in the intoxicating aroma of bronzing beans while sinking a freshly roasted espresso and gleaning pro-brewing tips.

We love to hear about your adventures in coffee, so make sure you tag us on Instagram.

Enjoy.

Kathryn Lewis
Editor
Indy Coffee Guides

@indycoffeeguide

HOW TO USE THE GUIDE

Cafes

Coffee shops and cafes where you can drink top-notch speciality coffee. We've split the guide into areas to help you find places near you.

Roasteries

Meet the leading speciality coffee roasters and discover where to source beans. Find them after the cafes in each area.

Maps

Every cafe and roastery has a number so you can find them either on the area map at the start of each section, or on the detailed city maps.

More good stuff

Discover **More good cups** and **More good roasteries** at the back of the book.

Short on space? Take the *North, Midlands & North Wales Independent Coffee Guide* with you on your travels with the new app. Find out more at:

indycoffee.guide/app

Follow us on Instagram:

@indycoffeeguide

Your adventures start here

Northumberland,
Tyne and Wear
& County Durham

Brew & Bite – Heaton

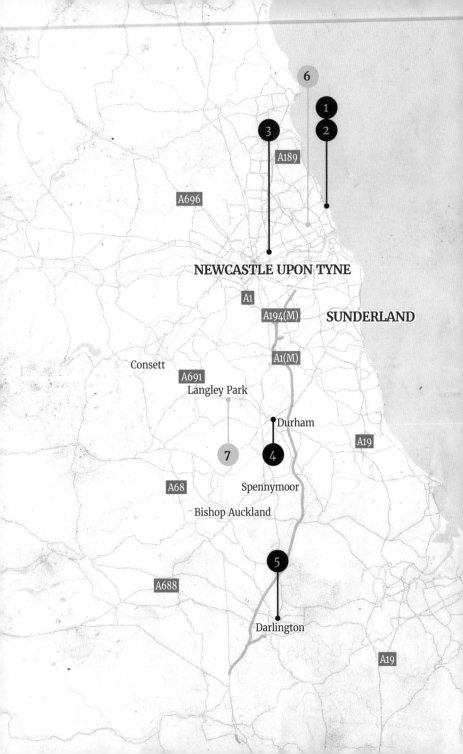

NEWCASTLE UPON TYNE

A189

A696

A1

A194(M)

SUNDERLAND

A1(M)

Consett

A691

Langley Park

Durham

A19

A68

Spennymoor

Bishop Auckland

A688

Darlington

A19

● CAFES

1   PureKnead
2   Rustic Cup
3   Brew & Bite – Heaton
4   Claypath Deli
5   Hatch Luncheonette

● ROASTERIES

6   Baristocracy Coffee
7   Fika Coffee Roasters

Find more good cafes and roasteries on pages 198–204

All locations are approximate

1 PUREKNEAD

111–113 Park View, Whitley Bay, Tyne and Wear, NE26 3RH

T ake a stroll along Park View and there's a good chance the waft of freshly baked pastries and just-ground coffee will draw you into this popular Whitley Bay venue.

PureKnead founder Paula Watson started selling her baked goods at Tynemouth Market in 2015. Her pastries, cakes and loaves were such a hit that two years later, when the opportunity arose to take over a former laundrette, she opened her first cafe-bakery.

 CHECK OUT PUREKNEAD 2.0 ON DEAN STREET IN NEWCASTLE

A daily haul of cinnamon-dusted buns, 48-hour sourdough loaves and crisp croissants has garnered a loyal fan base for the contemporary bakery. Make a lunchtime trip to devour homemade bagels and ciabatta stuffed with locally sourced artisan ingredients.

There's great coffee to be had, too. London's Square Mile provides a fab espresso blend and selection of single origins served as pourover or AeroPress. Whatever you plump for, pair it with a slab of traybake – the Fiery Dark Ginger slice is particularly tempting.

ESTABLISHED
2016

KEY ROASTER
Square Mile
Coffee Roasters

BREWING METHOD
Espresso,
AeroPress,
pourover

MACHINE
Victoria Arduino
White Eagle,
Victoria Arduino
Eagle One

GRINDER
Mythos One

OPENING HOURS
Tue–Sun
10am–2pm

Gluten FREE

BEANS AVAILABLE
INSTORE

WIFI

BRING YOUR OWN *Cup.*

DOG FRIENDLY

www.pure-knead.co.uk   07964 864181

f @purekneadwhitleybay   @purekneadwbay   @purekneadbakery

2 RUSTIC CUP

28 Park View, Whitley Bay, Tyne and Wear, NE26 2TH

For Rustic Cup founders Lee Coates and Veronika Pitakova it was a long road (both figuratively and literally) from their initial idea of opening a coffee shop to finally launching it.

The story started in Australia in 2017, where Lee and Veronika were inspired by the antipodean speciality coffee scene. They left Perth to begin the long journey back to the UK to set up their own cafe but, instead of flying the thousands of miles home, the pair set off on motorbikes.

 STICK AROUND FOR COCKTAILS, CRAFT BEER AND WINES ON FRIDAY AND SATURDAY NIGHTS

After experiencing a kaleidoscope of coffee cultures along the way, the duo finally arrived in the North East to open Rustic Cup in Whitley Bay in February 2020. The first year in business was a bumpy one as a result of the pandemic, but the venue has quickly established itself as a neighbourhood hangout for good coffee and sociable vibes.

Beans for the Sanremo machine are roasted nearby at Baristocracy, a roastery which shares similar inspirational Aussie origins. Choose between the house blend and a single origin, which can be prepared as espresso or filter.

ESTABLISHED
2020

KEY ROASTER
Baristocracy
Coffee Roasters

BREWING METHOD
Espresso, V60,
batch filter

MACHINE
Sanremo Café Racer

GRINDER
Mahlkonig Peak,
Mahlkonig EK43 S,
Mythos One

OPENING HOURS
Mon–Thu
7.30am–5pm
Fri–Sat
7.30am–10pm
Sun
9am–4pm

 Gluten FREE

 BEANS AVAILABLE INSTORE

 WIFI

 OUTDOOR seating

 DISABLED ACCESS

 BRING YOUR OWN Cup

 DOG FRIENDLY

www.rusticcup.co.uk   07379 134514
f @rusticcup.uk   🐦 @rusticcupuk   @rusticcup.uk

3 BREW & BITE – HEATON

214 Chillingham Road, Heaton, Newcastle upon Tyne, NE6 5LP

A huge floor-to-ceiling window lined with sourdough loaves, bags of coffee beans and drool-worthy pastries lures passersby into this neighbourhood hangout in the heart of Heaton. Bold blue and pink typography above the glass provides further kerb appeal should anyone miss the alluring carb and caffeine display.

Brew & Bite delivers exactly what it promises, and great coffee and delicious food share the star billing. So whether you're just popping in for a coffee to-go or stopping by for something to eat, there's a good chance you'll end up doing both.

 Insider's TIP GET A SECOND HELPING AT THE SISTER VENUE IN GOSFORTH

The team like to keep things fluid by having a multi-roaster approach to coffee. Two different espresso roasts are available at any time and usually include something from Hasbean in Staffordshire. Other recent faves have come from Redemption Roasters, Calendar Coffee, Square Mile and Workshop Coffee.

The bakes in the window aren't just for aesthetic purposes: the team put them to work in all-day dishes such as house toasties, brie-and-bacon-laced croissants, and crispy salt and chilli chicken stuffed brioche buns.

ESTABLISHED
2019

KEY ROASTER
Hasbean

BREWING METHOD
Espresso

MACHINE
Victoria Arduino Black Eagle

GRINDER
Victoria Arduino Mythos 2

OPENING HOURS
Mon–Fri
7.30am–6pm
Sat
8am–6pm
Sun
8.30am–4pm

 BEANS AVAILABLE / **INSTORE**

 WIFI

 OUTDOOR SEATING

 DOG FRIENDLY

www.brewandbitecoffee.co.uk   07802 273167

f @brewandbitecoffee   @ @brewandbite

4 CLAYPATH DELI

57 Claypath, Durham, County Durham, DH1 1QS

Good coffee and bread are two of life's simple but enjoyable pleasures, and at this Durham cafe-bakery a team of bakers and baristas excel in delivering fine examples of both.

For over ten years, the family set-up has been the source of beautiful sourdough loaves and top-notch coffee crafted at its Claypath home. Visitors can enjoy the fruits of the team's labours in the cosy cafe space, out in a leafy courtyard, or as a takeaway riverside feast.

MAKE A RETURN VISIT FOR ONE OF THE SOURDOUGH-PIZZA EVENINGS

Coffee beans served as espresso and batch filter are sourced from a collection of local roasteries. The current offering is roasted by Rounton in North Yorkshire and Durham newbie Fika.

The accompanying sourdough bakes don't just come in loaf form: a daily line-up of bagels, focaccia and pastries is available to eat in or take out. Claypath's homemade bagels are something of a local speciality and are stuffed with (local, where possible) ingredients such as cream cheese, avocado, tomatoes and crispy bacon.

ESTABLISHED
2010

KEY ROASTER
Rounton Coffee Roasters

BREWING METHOD
Espresso, batch filter

MACHINE
La Spaziale S5

GRINDER
Anfim Milano

OPENING HOURS
Tue-Sat
11am-4pm

 BEANS AVAILABLE

 INSTORE

 WIFI

 OUTDOOR SEATING

 DOG FRIENDLY

01913 407209
f @claypathdeli 🐦 @claypathdeli 📷 @claypath_deli

We are The Kore Directive.

We are a community of coffee people striving for greater inclusivity and accessibility within our industry.

LGBTQIA+ & POC friendly. Everyone is welcome.

We host both physical and virtual events for those who support our mission, with the aim to make the coffee industry representative for all.

Join the conversation:
www.thekoredirective.co.uk
@thekoredirective

5 HATCH LUNCHEONETTE

32 Blackwellgate, Darlington, County Durham, DL1 5HN

This Darlington find is a haven of ethically sourced coffee, incredible edibles, lush houseplants and all-round good vibes.

Husband-and-wife team Phil and Jasmin Robson spend their days in the Hatch kitchen where they whip up delectable brunch dishes using the freshest ingredients. Out front, the baristas craft espresso and filters lavished with Acorn Dairy milk from the organic farm that's just three miles away. If dairy isn't your thing, opt for Minor Figures' oat variety instead.

insider's TIP HEAD TO HATCH FOR A MEAN BLOODY MARY

Join those in the know and scoot upstairs to the first-floor seating area to enjoy a Rounton coffee and something scrumptious from the menu – curried puy lentils with falafel flatbread is a good shout. Loosen your belt and chase it with a slab of homemade strawberry and white-chocolate red velvet cake.

Upcoming thrills include the opening of HtchToGo next door, which'll specialise in takeout coffee, sarnies, cakes and Carpigiani soft-serve ice cream.

ESTABLISHED
2018

KEY ROASTER
Rounton Coffee Roasters

BREWING METHOD
Espresso, batch filter

MACHINE
Sanremo Café Racer

GRINDER
Fiorenzato F64 Evo

OPENING HOURS
Wed-Sun
9am-5pm

01325 380720
 @hatchluncheonette @hatchlunch @hatchluncheonette

Roasteries

Northumberland, Tyne and Wear & County Durham

6 BARISTOCRACY COFFEE

Unit 2 Larch Court, West Chirton North Industrial Estate, North Shields, Tyne and Wear, NE29 8SG

This family-run roastery aims to bring Australian-standard speciality coffee to the north east of England. Owner Alex Forsyth was born and raised in Sydney, where his father taught him how to roast and prepare coffee. In 2017 he moved to the UK with his partner Kate, who, along with their two children, helps run the business.

Baristocracy imports coffee from a variety of origins including Burundi, Colombia, Ethiopia, Democratic Republic of Congo, Honduras, Nicaragua, Rwanda and Uganda. Alex's main focus is on roasting flavour-forward single origins which he switches up regularly, depending on what's in season.

ESTABLISHED
2017

ROASTER MAKE & SIZE
Toper 15kg

'ALEX'S MAIN FOCUS IS ON ROASTING FLAVOUR-FORWARD SINGLE ORIGINS'

Coffee fans can sample Baristocracy beans at one of its local cafe customers or order them direct for delivery. The seasonal blend is particularly popular; the exact mix changes depending on what's tasting fresh and funky, but it's always something with bright, fruity, chocolatey and nutty notes.

During the pandemic, Alex and Kate upped the retail side of the business by stocking beans and equipment. Their coffee education courses are popular, too, and include the likes of Home Barista, Introduction to Professional Barista Skills, and Coffee Appreciation.

---

www.baristocracycoffee.com   **07908 007726**
f @baristocracycoffee   @baristocracy

7 FIKA COFFEE ROASTERS

Unit 2b, Riverside Industrial Estate, Langley Park, Durham, DH7 9TT

The name and branding of this new Durham roastery may scream Scandi but it was in fact the caffeine-mad city of Melbourne that inspired founders Matt Mitchell and Lynn Hepple to launch Fika.

During a six-year stint in Australia's caffeine capital, Matt trained as a barista and fell in love with the speciality craft. Back home in the North East, he and Lynn turned their passion into a career by investing in a 15kg Giesen in order to start roasting top-grade beans from across the world.

'COMMITTED TO MAKING THE ROASTING PROCESS AS TRANSPARENT AS POSSIBLE'

The duo are committed to making the roasting process as transparent as possible: they've already established direct-trade partnerships with farms in Brazil, Colombia and Uganda. They also open the roastery to the coffee-loving public Monday to Friday (12pm-2.30pm) so visitors can take a peek behind the scenes and pick up bags of beans to brew at home.

After just a year in business, Fika is already making a name for itself in the area – find it in the grinders of indie cafes, bars and restaurants across Durham.

ESTABLISHED
2020

ROASTER MAKE & SIZE
Giesen W15A
15kg

OPEN
TO THE PUBLIC

BEANS
AVAILABLE
ONLINE ONSITE

---

www.fikacoffeeroasters.co.uk   07702 569063

f @fikacoffeeroasters.co.uk   🐦 @fikacoffeeroast   📷 @fikacoffeeroasters

Cumbria, Lancashire & Merseyside

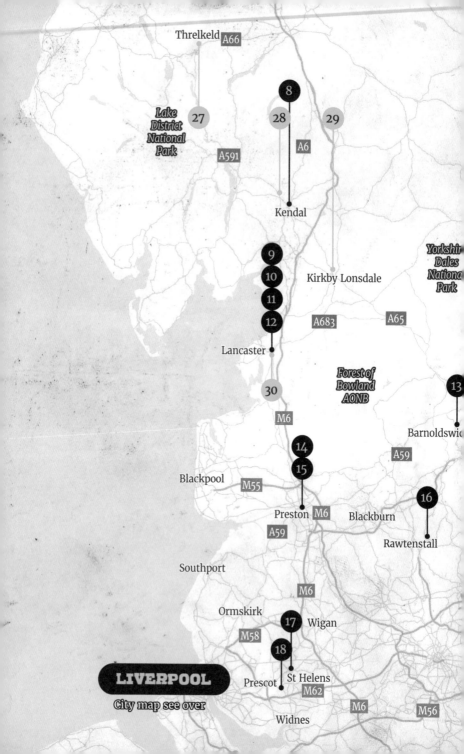

● CAFES

8   Comida [food]
9   Atkinsons The Castle
10 Atkinsons The Hall
11 Atkinsons The Music Room
12 Journey Social Kitchen
13 Frank Street Coffee House
14 Rise.
15 Cedarwood Coffee Company
16 Siphon Espresso & Brew Bar
17 Two Brothers – St Helens
18 Caffé & Co.

● ROASTERIES

27 Carvetii Coffee Roasters
28 Rinaldo's Speciality Coffee & Fine Tea
29 Kirkby Lonsdale Coffee Roasters
30 Atkinsons Shop and Roastery

Find more good cafes and roasteries on pages 198–204

All locations are approximate

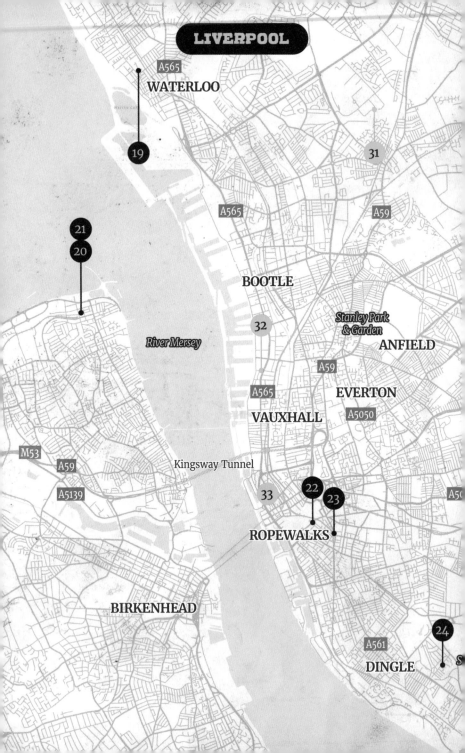

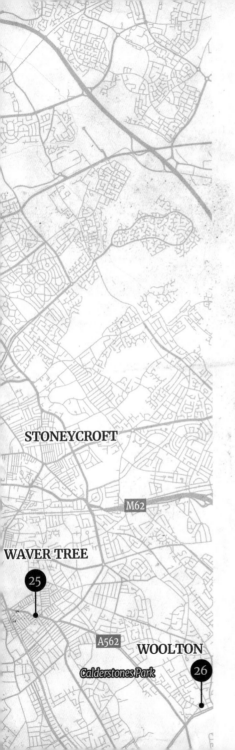

● CAFES

19 Crosby Coffee – Oxford Road
20 SUP
21 The Sea Shanty
22 Root Coffee
23 Bold Street Coffee
24 Crosby Coffee – Lark Lane
25 Bean There Coffee Shop
26 One Percent Forest

● ROASTERIES

31 Crosby Coffee Roasters
32 Neighbourhood Coffee
33 Django Coffee Co.

Find more good cafes and roasteries on pages 198–204

All locations are approximate

8 COMIDA [FOOD]

90 Highgate, Kendal, Cumbria, LA9 4HE

C umbria is the UK capital for adventure holidays, and at this Mediterranean-inspired cafe and restaurant in Kendal even tastebuds get to take a trip.

Comida [food] is owned by Yorkshireman Simon and Spaniard Alba, and the pair have created a venue to fortify both bold explorers and laidback holidaymakers via brunch and tapas menus influenced by Alba's heritage.

 Insider's TIP

REWARD YOUR ADVENTURES WITH A BALL BAGEL: MEATBALLS, TOMATO SAUCE AND MANCHEGO CHEESE

While the food menu is rooted in Spain, the coffee offering is inspired by Comida's Cumbrian setting: the house roast hails from Atkinsons in Lancaster, while guest beans are bronzed at down-the-road roastery Red Bank. For a continental take, try the Café Bombon special – a Valencian twist on espresso.

Tapas is undoubtedly the OG of sharing-style dining, and this cafe's menu of small dishes offers a feast of exciting flavours. Visit with friends who share an all-or-nothing approach to eating out, but be sure to leave room for a slice of the gluten-free Basque cheesecake.

Comida [food] was a finalist in *Cumbria Life*'s Reader Awards 2018 and lauded by *BBC Good Food* as one of the best places to eat in Cumbria. A sister venue is scheduled to open next door in late 2021.

ESTABLISHED
2017

KEY ROASTER
Atkinsons
Coffee Roasters

BREWING METHOD
Espresso, filter

MACHINE
Sanremo
Verona RS

GRINDER
Mythos One

OPENING HOURS
Wed-Fri
12pm-10pm
Sat
10am-10pm
Sun
10am-4pm

 Gluten FREE

 BEANS AVAILABLE INSTORE

 WIFI

 CYCLE FRIENDLY

 OUTDOOR SEATING

 DISABLED ACCESS

 BRING YOUR OWN Cup.

 DOG FRIENDLY

www.comidafood.co.uk   01539 732082
f @comidakendal   @comida_kendal   @comida_kendal

9 ATKINSONS THE CASTLE

Lancaster Castle, Castle Hill, Lancaster, Lancashire, LA1 1YN

ancaster Castle has dominated the city's skyline for nearly a millennium and now, following an extensive programme of restoration and renovation, it's become a major modern tourist attraction.

A sweeping piazza surrounded by recently uncovered cloisters, spruced-up turrets and the newly created Kitchen Courtyard is also home to another Lancastrian legend: Atkinsons Coffee Roasters.

IMMERSION DRIP FILTERS ARE A GREAT WAY TO DIVE INTO ATKINSONS' SINGLE-ORIGIN ROASTS

Visit to experience the stunning juxtaposition of 21st-century design with the original castle walls. The charm of the former prison-kitchen and additional contemporary room that make up the cafe space, combined with the roastery's rich coffee and tea heritage, result in an unforgettable experience.

Delicious pastries, bakes and sandwiches (crafted at the Bakery HQ on China Street and freshly prepared in-house) accompany a comprehensive menu of loose-leaf teas and own-roasted speciality coffee from one of the UK's pioneering roasteries.

Espresso, immersion drip, Chemex and batch brew are all on offer from the friendly and knowledgeable baristas, and can be enjoyed inside or in the spectacular castle courtyard.

ESTABLISHED
2019

KEY ROASTER
Atkinsons Coffee Roasters

BREWING METHOD
Espresso, Chemex, Hario V60 Immersion Dripper, batch brew

MACHINE
La Marzocco FB80

GRINDER
Mythos One, Mythos 2, Mahlkonig EK43

OPENING HOURS
Mon-Sun
10am-5pm

---

www.thecoffeehopper.com   01524 65470

f @lancastercastlecafe   @coffeehopper   @atkinsons.coffee

10 ATKINSONS THE HALL

10 China Street, Lancaster, Lancashire, LA1 1EX

For lovers of the finest brews and freshest bakes, it's hard to imagine anywhere better than Atkinsons' flagship venue The Hall. This 1930s former parish hall on China Street is in the heart of Atkinsons' Lancaster home territory and is nestled alongside its bakery, roastery, and coffee and tea emporium.

An arched ceiling, original plasterwork and Canadian-maple flooring encase a vast meeting space; it's a unique and inspiring setting in which to enjoy Atkinsons' superb coffee offerings at their freshest.

 GRAB A FRESHLY BAKED SOURDOUGH SANDWICH, CRAMMED WITH LOCALLY SOURCED FILLINGS

Skilled baristas prepare a dynamic selection of seasonal single origins and blends roasted mere steps away. One of just a few cafes to offer syphon as a prep method, The Hall team are particular about using the right brew methods to showcase the varied and intricate range of flavours within their extensive coffee menu.

No visit is complete without a peek at the adjoining roastery to discover the source of the delicious aromas, followed by a visit to the shop to check out the seductive array of beans for home brewing.

ESTABLISHED
2012

KEY ROASTER
Atkinsons
Coffee Roasters

BREWING METHOD
Espresso,
Chemex, syphon

MACHINE
Sanremo Café Racer

GRINDER
Mythos One
Clima Pro,
Mahlkonig EK43

OPENING HOURS
Mon–Fri
9am–4.30pm
Sat
9am–5pm
Sun
9.30am–4.30pm

Gluten FREE

WIFI

CYCLE FRIENDLY

BRING YOUR OWN Cup

DOG FRIENDLY

---

www.thecoffeehopper.com   **01524 65470**

f @thehallcafe   🐦 @coffeehopper   📷 @atkinsons.coffee

11 ATKINSONS THE MUSIC ROOM

Sun Square, Sun Street, Lancaster, Lancashire, LA1 1EW

The Music Room is to be discovered, after a little careful exploration, tucked away in Sun Square. This elegant coffee shop, housed within a Grade II-listed Georgian pavilion, is not only home to Atkinsons' beautiful brews; it also hosts art exhibitions and is the training ground for champion baristas.

Light floods through huge arched windows, cascading down white walls and infusing the wooden furnishings with the kind of soothing warmth that invites customers to linger.

 TEA LOVERS ARE JUST AS WELL LOOKED AFTER VIA A SPECIALIST LOOSE-LEAF COLLECTION

Choose from an array of Atkinsons single origins and blends, roasted just up the road at the China Street HQ and served as espresso and V60 at this sister site. On warm days, espresso tonic and cold brew are two of several delicious reasons to dip into the iced-coffee menu.

Whatever the weather, mezzanine-level indoor seating and sheltered outdoor tables and chairs provide somewhere to perch as you sip a coffee paired with cakes, bakes and sandwiches from Atkinsons' own artisan bakery.

ESTABLISHED
2010

KEY ROASTER
Atkinsons
Coffee Roasters

BREWING METHOD
Espresso, V60,
cold brew

MACHINE
Sanremo
Verona RS

GRINDER
Mythos One
Clima Pro

OPENING HOURS
Mon-Sat
10am-5pm
Sun
11am-4pm

 Gluten FREE

 BEANS AVAILABLE INSTORE

 WIFI

 CYCLE FRIENDLY

 OUTDOOR seating

 DISABLED ACCESS

 BRING YOUR OWN Cup

 DOG FRIENDLY

---

www.thecoffeehopper.com   01524 65470
f @themusicroomcafe   🐦 @coffeehopper   📷 @atkinsons.coffee

12 JOURNEY SOCIAL KITCHEN

28 New Street, Lancaster, Lancashire, LA1 1EG

Journey Social is somewhat of a brunch institution in Lancaster, so when this sister outpost opened on New Street in May 2021 Journey regulars were pretty jazzed.

The new digs were given a glow-up to match the contemporary styling of the original espresso bar, but benefit from having a bigger kitchen space (with an expanded kitchen team to match) and more room for indoor lounging, plus a bijou outdoor area.

IT'S ODDS ON THERE'LL BE A QUEUE WHEN YOU VISIT BUT, TRUST US, IT'S WORTH THE WAIT

There's plenty of room in which to road-test dishes from the drool-worthy brunch menu. Whether you plump for the JS staple of stacked-to-the-max french toast or go down the savoury route with the house-fave steak and eggs, you won't be disappointed. Everything is made from scratch and with a healthy dollop of care and attention.

Similar dedication to doing things properly is poured into the coffee offering. New Zealand's Allpress supplies the beans which are prepared as top-notch espresso and filter brews.

ESTABLISHED
2018

KEY ROASTER
Allpress Espresso

BREWING METHOD
Espresso, V60,
AeroPress

MACHINE
La Marzocco
Linea PB

GRINDER
Mythos One,
Mahlkonig EK43

OPENING HOURS
Mon–Sat
9am–5pm
Sun
9.30am–4pm

Gluten FREE

CYCLE FRIENDLY

OUTDOOR seating

DISABLED ACCESS

BRING YOUR OWN Cup.

COFFEE COURSES

DOG FRIENDLY

www.journeysocial.co.uk

@journeysocial1   @journeysociallancaster

13 FRANK STREET COFFEE HOUSE

12 Newtown, Barnoldswick, Lancashire, BB18 5UQ

A s the first and only independent takeaway coffee shop in Barnoldswick, Frank Street Coffee House's brews were a long-awaited and instant hit with caffeine-loving locals.

It's a small unit with no seating, but good things do indeed come in small packages where Frank Street is concerned. The house espresso blend and decaf option are roasted nearby by the excellent Atkinsons Coffee Roasters in Lancaster, so the coffee is always top-quality and uber fresh.

 ### PICK UP HUSKEE REUSABLE CUPS AND BREWING PARAPHERNALIA FROM THE RETAIL SELECTION

The team recently introduced a full CBD range, including oils that customers can buy and experiment with at home. You can also ask for 100 per cent organically grown hemp (known as hatcha) to be mixed into your latte, cappuccino, mocha, hot chocolate or americano for an extra pick-me-up.

Local bakery Cocoa Beans provides delicious cakes and traybakes to accompany the specialist drinks. The chunky Biscoff brownies and millionaire's slices are the most popular sugar-hit coffee pairings.

ESTABLISHED
2019

KEY ROASTER
Atkinsons
Coffee Roasters

BREWING METHOD
Espresso

MACHINE
Expobar G10

GRINDER
Mahlkonig,
Fiorenzato

OPENING HOURS
Mon
8am-3pm
Tue-Fri
8am-4pm
Sat
8am-1pm

 BEANS AVAILABLE INSTORE

 CYCLE FRIENDLY

 OUTDOOR Seating

 BRING YOUR OWN Cup.

 DOG FRIENDLY

www.frankstreetcoffee.co.uk   07725 550222
f @frankstreetcoffeehouse   @frankstreetcof1   @frankstreetcoffeehouse

14 RISE.

15 Miller Arcade, Preston, Lancashire, PR1 2QY

This Preston coffee house is out to prove that brunch is much more than just a midway meal. Whether it's the opportunity to spend quality time with someone special or simply treating oneself to a moment of peace – while scoffing something delicious, of course – the Rise team treat the between-breakfast-and-lunch ritual as something sacred.

Prepare yourself for a photo-ready, all-day menu. Breakfast rolls stuffed with inventive fillings offer an easy option for those who like to play it safe, while Feel Good Bowls bursting with fresh and nourishing ingredients send a siren call to the wellness crowd. Seasoned brunchers, meanwhile, will find it impossible to resist Brunch Club staples such as turkish eggs, and cherry and almond french toast.

NO TIME TO STOP? GET A COFFEE TO-GO FROM THE TAKEOUT HATCH

Everyone knows that a brunch pic for the IG grid isn't complete without a rosetta-adorned flat white artfully placed next to the dish. Thankfully, the coffees aren't just an aesthetically pleasing prop here as beans from Ozone Coffee Roasters guarantee delicious accompanying brews.

ESTABLISHED
2018

KEY ROASTER
Ozone Coffee Roasters

BREWING METHOD
Espresso, cold brew

MACHINE
La Marzocco Linea PB

GRINDER
Mazzer Kold

OPENING HOURS
Mon-Fri
8am-5pm
Sat-Sun
9am-5pm

www.risebrunch.co.uk
f @risebrunch   @risebrunch

15 CEDARWOOD COFFEE COMPANY

10 Winckley Street, Preston, Lancashire, PR1 2AA

C edarwood Coffee sits on one of Preston's pretty cobbled sidestreets, just a minute or so from the main shopping thoroughfare.

It's a relaxed two-storey cafe with great coffee – and a few places to enjoy it. Sit indoors, nurse a cup out on the cobbles or order at the ground-floor window bar or dedicated coffee-to-go queue and head to a nearby park.

 AFTERNOON VISIT? FOLLOW YOUR COFFEE WITH A COLD ONE FROM THE CRAFT BEER FRIDGE

House coffee Penny Rock comes from Kendal's Red Bank Coffee Roasters, and reveals smooth notes of buttery toffee when prepared as espresso. It's accompanied by a rotating range of single origins from a number of northern roasteries. Punters can also purchase retail beans for home brewing.

Coffee isn't only served hot at Cedarwood, and the team have built a reputation for their espresso-laced salted caramel milkshakes and vanilla-ice-cream affogatos. Both are sweet, moreish and not to be missed – as are the bakes on the stripped-down menu.

ESTABLISHED
2015

KEY ROASTER
Red Bank
Coffee Roasters

BREWING METHOD
Espresso, V60,
pourover,
Clever Dripper

MACHINE
Sanremo

GRINDER
Sanremo

OPENING HOURS
Mon–Sat
10am–5pm
Sun
11am–5pm
(seasonal opening hours)

 BEANS AVAILABLE INSTORE

 WIFI

 CYCLE FRIENDLY

 OUTDOOR SEATING

 BRING YOUR OWN CUP

---

www.cedarwood.coffee   03333 034352

f @cedarwoodcoffee   🐦 @winckleystreet   📷 @cedarwoodcoffee

16 SIPHON ESPRESSO & BREW BAR

91 Bank Street, Rawtenstall, Rossendale, Lancashire, BB4 7QN

There aren't many places in Lancashire where you get coffee prepared via syphon (or siphon, as it's also spelt), so if you're yet to watch the hypnotic prep method it's worth making a trip to this cafe named in its honour.

The mesmerising syphon is just one of a comprehensive range of brewing methods used at this specialist coffee bar. Espresso is, of course, the most popular option, but founder Scott Moore also offers V60, drip and cold brew.

INSIDER'S TIP: FOUR-PAWED PATRONS ARE SPOILED ROTTEN WITH FREE DOG TREATS

The raw materials are sourced from a variety of Northern roasters and the current line-up revolves around roasts from Crosby Coffee in Liverpool and Abe & Co. in Greater Manchester. Ask Scott or one of the baristas for their recommended pairing of coffee type and prep method.

There's an impressive selection of homemade bakes on the bar which makes popping in purely for coffee almost impossible. A small menu of staple dishes (think sausage ciabattas and toasted banana bread with mascarpone and blueberries) offers heartier options for breakfast and lunch visits.

ESTABLISHED
2018

KEY ROASTER
Crosby Coffee

BREWING METHOD
Espresso, syphon, V60, cold brew

MACHINE
Sanremo Verona RS

GRINDER
Eureka Mythos, Eureka Zenith, Eureka Drogheria

OPENING HOURS
Mon–Fri
9am–4pm
Sat
9.30am–4pm
Sun
10am–4pm

Gluten FREE

BEANS AVAILABLE
INSTORE

WIFI

CYCLE FRIENDLY

OUTDOOR SEATING

DISABLED ACCESS

BRING YOUR OWN Cup

DOG FRIENDLY

01706 830893

f @siphonespressobrewbar   🐦 @siphonespresso1   📷 @siphonespressobrewbar

17 TWO BROTHERS – ST HELENS

6 Ormskirk Street, Globe Buildings, St Helens, Merseyside, WA10 1BH

The newest member of the Two Brothers family, this St Helens outpost opened on the ground floor of the gorgeous Globe Buildings in August 2021.

Unlike the OG Altrincham venue with its all-black interior, the new coffee shop is light and spacious thanks to sweeping curved floor-to-ceiling windows. Inside, white walls, bleached wood and tumbling houseplants create a contemporary space to chill out, meet friends and drink great coffee.

 LOOK OUT FOR TWO BROTHERS 4.0 WHICH'LL BE POPPING UP AT THE BOOKSHOP ACROSS THE ROAD

Beans for the line-up of espresso and filter drinks are bronzed by head roaster Sean at the Two Brothers roastery-cafe in Warrington. He picks seasonal lots based on flavour, sustainability and a fair price being paid to farmers. The single-origin offering changes regularly, so ask the baristas what they recommend.

If the sun's shining, order an iced latte and take it alfresco to enjoy on the sunny south-facing patio. In colder months, cosy up on the banquette seating or take a perch at the window bar.

ESTABLISHED
2021

KEY ROASTER
Two Brothers

BREWING METHOD
Espresso, V60,
batch brew

MACHINE
La Marzocco FB80

GRINDER
Mythos One,
Mahlkonig EK43

OPENING HOURS
Mon–Fri
7am–5pm
Sat
8am–5pm
Sun
10am–4pm

 Gluten FREE

 BEANS AVAILABLE INSTORE

 WIFI

 CYCLE FRIENDLY

 OUTDOOR seating

 DISABLED ACCESS

 BRING YOUR OWN Cup

 DOG FRIENDLY

www.twobrothers.coffee
f @twobrotherscoffeeltd 🐦 @2btwobrothers 📷 @twobrotherscoffee

18 CAFFÈ & CO.

8 Dane Court, Rainhill, Prescot, Merseyside, L35 4LU

When it was established in 2011, Caffè & Co. was one of the first speciality coffee shops in the North West. During its decade in business it's branched out and now offers SCA training as well as roasting its own coffee under the brand Rainhill Coffee Roasters.

Own-roasted beans take the lead on the coffee menu, but visitors will also find a rotating selection of guest roasters which often includes Hasbean, Atkinsons and Gardelli. There's a good range of brewing options available, so ask owner and coffee pro Neil Osthoff which method he'd recommend for your pick of the beans.

 BRUSH UP YOUR BARISTA SKILLS AT THE IN-HOUSE SCA TRAINING SCHOOL

It's not all about the coffee: the food is also wow-worthy. Try a stack of buttermilk pancakes with sweet toppings or chunky waffles draped in the best parts of a full English. Those with an optimistic appetite should take on the Pulled Pork Burger XL – two 6oz steak burgers, glazed pulled-pork, back bacon, lettuce, tomato and Swiss cheese on a sourdough bun, plus fries, slaw and beer-battered onion rings.

Visit at the weekend to make the most of the newly extended opening hours and alcohol licence.

ESTABLISHED
2011

KEY ROASTER
Rainhill Coffee Roasters

BREWING METHOD
Espresso, V60, AeroPress, french press

MACHINE
La Marzocco Linea PB

GRINDER
Anfim

OPENING HOURS
Mon–Thu
8am–4.30pm
Fri
8am–9pm
Sat
9am–9pm
Sun
9.30am–9pm
(seasonal hours, check website)

 Gluten FREE

 BEANS AVAILABLE INSTORE

 WIFI

 CYCLE FRIENDLY

 OUTDOOR seating

 DISABLED ACCESS

 BRING YOUR OWN Cup

 COFFEE COURSES

www.caffeandco.com 01514 932332

f @caffeandco 🐦 @caffeandco 📷 @caffe_and_co

19 CROSBY COFFEE – OXFORD ROAD

2 Oxford Road, Waterloo, Liverpool, Merseyside, L22 8QF

2021 proved to be a busy year for Crosby Coffee co-owners Jack Foster and Mark Slinger who, alongside opening a new venue in Aigburth, made extensive renovations to their original cafe on Oxford Road.

Since opening in 2017, the Waterloo coffee shop has garnered a loyal following of caffeine fans who visit for own-roasted beans and good vibes. They've been rewarded with a refurb that includes the addition of a new "work from home" area downstairs where they can set up laptops and fuel Teams meetings with top-notch coffee and locally crafted pastries.

 LIMITED-EDITION SINGLE ORIGINS AND BLENDS KEEP THE COFFEE OFFERING FRESH

Other draws include weekly workshops such as Manual Brewing, Sensory Cupping, and Espresso & Latte Art, which give budding baristas the opportunity to brush up their skills. There's also an awesome range of coffee beans, equipment, merch and accessories available to buy in store (and online).

Check out the cafe's Independents Corner where the Crosby crew let three new and local indie businesses, which don't have premises, showcase their wares to the public.

ESTABLISHED
2017

KEY ROASTER
Crosby Coffee

BREWING METHOD
Espresso, V60, AeroPress

MACHINE
Custom Conti Monte Carlo Ultima

GRINDER
Compak E5, Compak E6, Compak E8, Mahlkonig EK43

OPENING HOURS
Mon-Fri
8am-4.30pm
Sat-Sun
9am-4pm

 Gluten FREE

 BEANS AVAILABLE INSTORE

 WIFI

 CYCLE FRIENDLY

 OUTDOOR SEATING

 DISABLED ACCESS

 BRING YOUR OWN Cup

 COFFEE COURSES

 DOG FRIENDLY

---

www.crosbycoffee.co.uk   01515 385454

f @crosbycoffee   🐦 @crosbycoffeeltd   @ @crosbycoffeeltd

great **taste** PRODUCER

CAKESMITHS

GREAT COFFEE SHOPS DESERVE GREAT CAKE.

TRY US FOR FREE IN YOUR COFFEE SHOP!

- Award-winning wholesale cakes
- Top-notch coffee shop solutions
- Loyalty points and free cake
- Unrivalled cake innovation from our Cake Lab

- Next day delivery, 6 days a week
- Hints and tips to sell more cake
- Eco-friendly packaging
- Everything made by hand

Try us for free at cakesmiths.com/try-us

@cakesmiths.hq

20 SUP

6 Atherton Street, New Brighton, Merseyside, CH45 2NY

No-one could judge you for popping into SUP for a quick latte only to leave with a beautifully designed print and a cheeky take-out tipple, as Luce and Scott's coffee/gift/bottle-shop-meets-print-studio is a cathedral to caffeine and design.

SUP stands for 'Shop, Unwind, Print' and Luce and Scott wanted to be a SUPplier of crafted goods and a SUPporter of talented makers while also creating an intimate place to quaff coffee, craft beer, fine cider and natural wine.

 VISIT FOR TASTER EVENINGS, MEET-THE-MAKERS EVENTS AND SHORT COURSES

The pair have clocked up impressive barista experience (Scott worked in cafes across the Wirral while Luce has pulled espressos all around Australia) so they see to it that Bon Bon beans from Hundred House are prepped for optimum flavour. They can also advise on the best coffees to brew at home from the retail selection.

Behind the smart La Marzocco, shelves of bottles and craftwork you'll discover Toucan Tango, where the couple showcase talents for bold and bright print design.

ESTABLISHED
2020

KEY ROASTER
Hundred
House Coffee

BREWING METHOD
Espresso

MACHINE
La Marzocco
Linea Classic

GRINDER
Anfim Caimano
On Demand

OPENING HOURS
Wed-Sat
10am-9pm
Sun
10am-5pm

 Gluten FREE

 BEANS AVAILABLE
 INSTORE

 WIFI

 OUTDOOR SEATING

 DISABLED ACCESS

  DOG FRIENDLY

www.wearesupshop.com   07545 138081
f @wearesup   🐦 @wearesup   📷 @wearesupshop

21 THE SEA SHANTY

4 Atherton Street, Wallasey, Merseyside, CH45 2NY

The good vibes come from more than just the quality coffee at this New Brighton coffee house, thanks to The Sea Shanty's ethos of giving back to the community.

Not only do all tips get donated to local charities, but the team have also introduced a Coffee for a Stranger concept where customers pay forward a drink for someone in need. The Sea Shanty hosts regular workshops and events, too, such as the Friday Lunchtime Sessions, Saturday Shanty Jams, art workshops and afternoon board games.

 ### THE SHANTY GARDEN PROVIDES ALFRESCO SEATING FOR SUNNY DAYS

Beans fuelling the various activities are roasted in Birkenhead by the pros at Adams + Russell. Sample the rich notes of the house espresso in a flat white made with Peckforton Farm Dairy milk or one of the range of barista-standard plant-based alternatives. Pair it with a slice of homemade vegan cake, or take the luxe up a notch via an affogato crafted from silky espresso and Cornish ice cream (there's also a plant-based option).

ESTABLISHED
2018

KEY ROASTER
Adams + Russell

BREWING METHOD
Espresso, V60

MACHINE
Expobar G10

GRINDER
Noveseinove 969
On-Demand

OPENING HOURS
Wed–Sun
10am–4pm

Gluten FREE

BEANS AVAILABLE
INSTORE

 WIFI

 CYCLE FRIENDLY

 OUTDOOR seating

 BRING YOUR OWN Cup

 DOG FRIENDLY

22 ROOT COFFEE

52 Hanover Street, Liverpool, Merseyside, L1 4AF

Filter fans are guaranteed to find something to excite them on the drinks list at this Liverpool coffee bar.

The rabble of Root baristas love nothing more than getting their hands on a new bag of beans and experimenting to find the perfect V60 and Chemex recipes to share with their loyal following.

THERE'S PLENTY OF SEATING INSIDE AND OUT, SO FEEL FREE TO WHIP OUT A LAPTOP OR BOOK

Craft House Coffee in Sussex has been the roaster of choice for a few years now and, alongside guests Hundred House and Hard Beans, sends the team a seasonal selection of single origins to explore.

While the coffee menu is comprehensive, the Root team are great at making everyone feel welcome – wherever they are on their coffee journey.

'We love a chat and the chance to engage with our customers; it's amazing to see an interest in speciality coffee being sparked for the first time,' says manager Jasmine Nevitt.

Jasmine and fellow manager Michael Hollywood have recently stripped back the food menu, enabling them to focus on sourcing local ingredients and making as much in-house as possible. This new direction mirrors the care and attention that goes into the coffee offering.

ESTABLISHED
2015

KEY ROASTER
Craft House Coffee

BREWING METHOD
Espresso, Chemex, batch brew, V60

MACHINE
Victoria Arduino Black Eagle Gravimetric

GRINDER
Nuova Simonelli Mythos One, Nuova Simonelli Mythos 2, Mahlkonig EK43

OPENING HOURS
Mon–Sun
10am–5pm

 Gluten FREE

 BEANS AVAILABLE INSTORE

 WIFI

 OUTDOOR SEATING

 DISABLED ACCESS

 COFFEE COURSES

 DOG FRIENDLY

---

www.rootcoffee.co.uk   01517 084995

f @rootcoffeeliv   🐦 @rootcoffeeliv   📷 @rootcoffeeliv

23 BOLD STREET COFFEE

89 Bold Street, Liverpool, Merseyside, L1 4HF

Since 2010, Bold Street Coffee has brought people together around cafe tables and turntables. Old-school vinyl spins a soundtrack to the lively comings and goings of the locals who flock here each day.

Bold Street not only has the community at its heart but is also at the heart of the community. Lockdown takeaway queues flowed down the street and the successful Ain't No Time to Hate art exhibition raised over £7,000 for the Anthony Joshua Foundation.

 Insider's TIP A NEW SISTER SITE IS DUE TO OPEN ON MANCHESTER'S CROSS STREET AT THE END OF 2021

Relationships are forged over brews, doughnuts and Buoys – BSC's trademark brioche bun creation, which was named at a nautical pop-up event (and in recognition of the height of the super-stacked breakfast burgers). Expect generous proportions of both scran and good times.

A quarterly rotation of guest roasts from the likes of Dark Arts, The Barn and Red Bank keeps the coffee offering interesting. Fruity, punchy guest espressos are chosen to contrast with the mellow and chocolatey house beans, which the Bold Street team roast in the city in collaboration with Crosby Coffee.

ESTABLISHED
2010

KEY ROASTER
Bold Street Coffee

BREWING METHOD
Espresso,
batch brew

MACHINE
La Marzocco
Linea PB

GRINDER
Nuova Simonelli
Mythos One,
Nuova Simonelli
Mythos 2

OPENING HOURS
Mon–Sat
8am–6pm
Sun
9am–5pm

 BEANS AVAILABLE INSTORE

 WIFI

 CYCLE FRIENDLY

 OUTDOOR SEATING

 BRING YOUR OWN CUP.

 DOG FRIENDLY

www.boldstreetcoffee.co.uk   01517 097172

f @bold.streetcoffee   🐦 @boldstcoffee   📷 @boldstreetcoffee

24 CROSBY COFFEE – LARK LANE

62 Lark Lane, Aigburth, Liverpool, Merseyside, L17 8UP

This new opening by Jack Foster and Mark Slinger is the next chapter in the Crosby Coffee success story.

As at the pair's original cafe on Oxford Road, coffee takes centre stage at Lark Lane where four grinders, crammed with own-roasted single origins, blends and decafs, keep all the options open for coffee connoisseurs.

If you're a sucker for roasted hazelnut and chocolate notes, try the Iron Men blend (named after sculptor Antony Gormley's 100 cast-iron figures on Crosby Beach) made with beans from Brazil, Honduras and Guatemala.

ASK THE SCA-TRAINED BARISTAS WHAT'S AVAILABLE IN THE FOUR GRINDERS

The food offering is a simple but delicious selection of artisan sandwiches and award-winning cakes and cookies from local bakery Dumb Dough. Pastries supplied by The Butterholic in Kirkby are also seriously good, particularly the house fave: chocolate-drizzled croissants.

A "work from home" laptop space proved such a hit at Oxford Road that Jack and Mark have made room for a similar set-up in the basement here, so customers can work and slurp from dawn till dusk.

ESTABLISHED
2021

KEY ROASTER
Crosby Coffee

BREWING METHOD
Espresso, V60,
AeroPress

MACHINE
Custom Conti
Monte Carlo Ultima

GRINDER
Compak E5,
Compak E6,
Compak E8,
Mahlkonig EK43

OPENING HOURS
Mon-Fri
8am–5pm
Sat-Sun
9am–4pm

 Gluten FREE

 BEANS AVAILABLE INSTORE

 WIFI

 OUTDOOR seating

 DISABLED ACCESS

 BRING YOUR OWN Cup

 COFFEE COURSES

 DOG FRIENDLY

---

www.crosbycoffee.co.uk   01515 385454

 @crosbycoffee   @crosbycoffeeltd   @crosbycoffeeltd

25 BEAN THERE COFFEE SHOP

376 Smithdown Road, Liverpool, Merseyside, L15 5AN

Since setting up shop on the corner of Penny Lane in 2017, Bean There has become a busy hub of neighbourhood activity in Liverpool's southside.

An eclectic schedule of events – ranging from *Great British Bake Off*-watching parties to spoken-word performances and acoustic live-music nights – has put the sociable coffee shop at the heart of the community.

 KEEP 'EM PEELED: A SISTER CAFE AND BAKERY WILL BE OPENING SOON

When the Bean There crew aren't hosting out-of-hours events, they're crafting artisan coffee and delicious food for their loyal following of regulars and visitors. Lancaster roastery Atkinsons is their long-term coffee partner and, alongside local roastery Neighbourhood, supplies top-notch beans for the La Marzocco Linea PB and brewing paraphernalia.

The busy little kitchen crafts a huge range of breakfasts, Buddha bowls and homemade bakes. Picking up lunch to eat alfresco in one of the nearby parks? Try a Bean There sausage roll, choosing from the daily range which includes veggie and vegan editions such as the Middle Eastern-inspired cauliflower roll.

ESTABLISHED
2017

KEY ROASTER
Atkinsons
Coffee Roasters

BREWING METHOD
Espresso, V60,
Chemex,
batch brew,
cold brew

MACHINE
La Marzocco
Linea PB

GRINDER
Victoria Arduino
Mythos One

OPENING HOURS
Mon-Fri
8am-5pm
Sat-Sun
9am-5pm

www.beantherecoffeeshop.com   01517 332324

f @beantherecoffeeshop   🐦 @beanthere_lpl   📷 @beantherecoffeeshop

26 ONE PERCENT FOREST

42 Allerton Road, Woolton, Liverpool, Merseyside, L25 7RG

While many speciality cafe owners owe their inspiration to Australasian coffee culture, the couple who launched One Percent Forest have Iceland to thank for their Liverpool coffee shop.

After falling in love with Icelandic culture on their travels, Hannah and Dean wanted to recreate the experience back home in Woolton. And, thanks to a successful crowdfunding campaign, they were able to open One Percent Forest in 2018. The pared-back interior dressed with bleached wood, houseplants and Polaroids encapsulates signature Scandi styling, while retail bags of beans from Reykjavik Roasters nod to Hannah and Dean's time in Iceland.

CHECK OUT THE LINE-UP OF NATURAL WINES, CRAFT BEERS AND COCKTAILS

Sustainability is a priority for the duo and recent eco updates include sourcing beans in reusable tubs from Dark Woods, and using milk from Brades Farm in Lancashire. The result is an indulgent line-up of espresso drinks made using irresistibly silky steamed milk.

A unique brunch and lunch menu, featuring the likes of waffles topped with blueberries, skyr yogurt, lingonberry jam and agave, and hot dogs with pickles, dill mustard, remoulade and crispy onions, completes the Nordic experience.

ESTABLISHED
2018

KEY ROASTER
Dark Woods Coffee

BREWING METHOD
Espresso, batch filter, cold brew

MACHINE
La Marzocco Linea AV

GRINDER
Victoria Arduino Mythos One

OPENING HOURS
Mon–Thu, Sun
10am–4pm
Fri–Sat
10am–11pm

 Gluten FREE

 BEANS AVAILABLE INSTORE

 WIFI

 OUTDOOR seating

 BRING YOUR OWN Cup

DOG FRIENDLY

www.onepercentforest.co.uk   01514 281425

f @onepercentforest   🐦 @1percentforest   📷 @onepercentforest

Roasteries

Cumbria, Lancashire & Merseyside

27 CARVETII COFFEE ROASTERS

Unit 3c, Threlkeld Business Park, Threlkeld, Cumbria, CA12 4SU

C arvetii celebrated its tenth birthday in 2021, marking a decade at the heart of all things coffee in Cumbria.

During this time, it's been the worthy recipient of several industry awards and earned a reputation for its unstinting commitment to supporting its stockists and customers – via training, accreditation, technical advice and hands-on machinery maintenance.

'A REPUTATION FOR ITS UNSTINTING COMMITMENT TO SUPPORTING ITS STOCKISTS AND CUSTOMERS'

Head roaster Angharad MacDonald and her team are on a never-ending quest to find exceptional beans. It's a journey that sees them sourcing from the world's best growers and, in 2021, led them to forge an exclusive and sustainable partnership – their first– with Colombian farm Casa Loma.

The roastery usually has six roasts on the go at any one time (a couple of distinctive espresso blends, three single origins for filter, and a decaf option) ensuring there's always a good brew available at the North West's finest coffee shops.

ESTABLISHED
2011

ROASTER MAKE & SIZE
Probatone 25kg
Probat UC12
12kg

OPEN
BY APPOINTMENT

COFFEE
COURSES

COURSES

BEANS
AVAILABLE

ONLINE

---

www.carvetiicoffee.co.uk   **01768 776979**

f @carvetiicoffee   🐦 @carvetiicoffee   📷 @carvetiicoffee

28 RINALDO'S SPECIALITY COFFEE & FINE TEA

Unit 12, Lakeland Food Park (Plumgarths), Kendal, Cumbria, LA8 8QJ

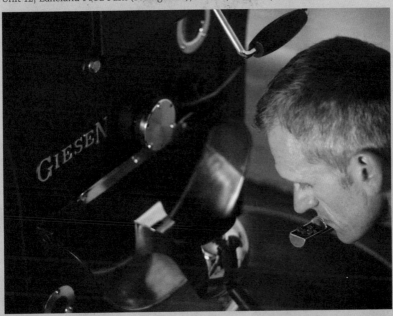

Since it was established in 2015, Rinaldo's has roasted beans from every coffee-growing country in the world.

Sourcing beans direct from producers and through trusted importers, the team (headed up by founder Rinaldo Colombi) test-roast in their Ikawa Pro before upscaling the precise recipe for the chunky Giesen W15. High standards are paramount and, in 2020, earned the roastery a Great Taste award for its Casa Espresso Blend.

'COFFEE FANS CAN VISIT THE RECENTLY EXPANDED ROASTERY'

Coffee fans can visit the recently expanded roastery, which sits on the edge of Kendal in the Lake District National Park. The two floors open to the public contain professional facilities for barista training, a retail area (selling freshly roasted single-origin coffees, fine loose-leaf teas and brewing equipment) and an espresso bar for takeaway drinks.

ESTABLISHED
2015

ROASTER MAKE & SIZE
Giesen W15A
15kg
Ikawa Pro

CAFE ONSITE

COFFEE COURSES

BEANS AVAILABLE

www.rinscoffee.com   01539 592587

f @rinscoffee   🐦 @rinscoffee   📷 @rinscoffee

29 KIRKBY LONSDALE COFFEE ROASTERS

The Royal Barn, New Road, Kirkby Lonsdale, Cumbria, LA6 2AB

Beer heads and bean buffs work side by side at The Royal Barn, where two top-quality indie beverage businesses unite under one roof. Their owner, brewing and roasting multitasker Stu Taylor, maintains the highest standards when it comes to both hops and greens.

Formerly known as Kircabi Roasters, the crew at Kirkby Lonsdale Coffee Roasters continue in their mission to source and roast the freshest and most exciting single-origin coffees from across the globe. Recent hauls hail from Costa Rica, Brazil, Ethiopia, Indonesia, El Salvador, Colombia and Peru.

ESTABLISHED
2016

ROASTER MAKE & SIZE
Toper 5kg

CAFE
ONSITE

BEANS
AVAILABLE

'VISIT THE CUMBRIAN ROASTERY TO SAMPLE FRESH-FROM-THE-ROASTER BEANS'

The team also craft a selection of killer blends including Royal (notes of smooth choc with a fruity finish), Singletrack Deadline (a blast of smoky intensity) and Ride and Shine (a medium easy-drinker) – all of which are worthy of a slot at your next cupping sesh.

Visit the Cumbrian roastery to sample fresh-from-the-roaster beans while relishing the aromas of exotic greens being bronzed, then pop into the taphouse next door to explore the brewery's range of craft beers.

www.klbrewery.com 01524 271918
f @klbrewery @kirkbylonsdalecoffeeroasters

30 ATKINSONS SHOP AND ROASTERY

12 China Street, Lancaster, Lancashire, LA1 1EX

Atkinsons' fascinating heritage dates back to 1837, when tea, coffee, sugar and spices made their way from all over the globe to St George's Quay in Lancaster. The company's rich legacy is now honoured by current owners Ian and Sue Steel.

Fuelled by their passion for coffee and enormous respect for Atkinsons' history, Ian and Sue have successfully reinvigorated the brand to build a new generation of coffee lovers. As pioneers in the UK speciality coffee scene, they've also inspired a whole host of cafe owners, baristas and fellow independent roasteries.

'PIONEERS IN THE UK SPECIALITY COFFEE SCENE, THEY'VE INSPIRED A GENERATION'

Their own roastery – hidden behind Atkinsons' enchanting coffee and tea emporium and The Hall cafe on Lancaster's China Street– is steeped in eco-friendly practices. A clean, green Loring Kestrel sits alongside old-school Whitmee roasters, and Ian proactively nurtures Relationship Coffee partnerships with farmers.

Attention to detail is at the heart of the operation, and it shows in the quality of the coffee. Find it served at speciality cafes across the country, as well as at Atkinsons' own clutch of coffee shops in the city and at Mackie Mayor in Manchester.

ESTABLISHED
1837

ROASTER MAKE & SIZE
Loring Kestrel 35kg
Whitmee 56lb
Whitmee 28lb
Uno 14lb
Uno 7lb

CAFE ONSITE

OPEN BY APPOINTMENT

COFFEE COURSES

BEANS AVAILABLE
ONLINE ONSITE

---

www.thecoffeehopper.com   01524 65470
f @atkinsonscoffee   🐦 @coffeehopper   📷 @atkinsons.coffee

★ ★ single origin ★ ★
hot chocolate

Kokoa Collection is an award winning hot chocolate company sourcing cocoa beans from around the world. Choose from our nine single origins including vegan, organic and Fairtrade options.

Look out for your favourite in cafés or pick up a bag to enjoy at home. And please get in touch if you would like to serve Kokoa Collection in your café.

@kokoacollection

www.kokoacollection.co.uk
info@kokoacollection.co.uk
tel 0208 883 2660

hot chocolate
KOKOA
COLLECTION™
by origin

31 CROSBY COFFEE ROASTERS

Unit 3, Lockwoods Trading Estate, Bridle Way, Liverpool, Merseyside, L30 4UA

Jack Foster started Crosby Coffee from his mum's living room, turning his hobby into a business in 2014 when he established a professional roastery. Three years later, schoolfriend Mark Slinger came on board as business partner.

Together they've built an impressive commercial customer base, supplying Liverpool-roasted beans to hundreds of cafes, restaurants and businesses across the UK and Europe. In 2017, to keep up with demand, Crosby HQ relocated to a roastery-cafe in Waterloo.

'JACK AND MARK INTRODUCED A DEDICATED SUSTAINABILITY TEAM'

Crosby Coffee is one of just a handful of UK roasteries to offer a worldwide subscription service, so coffee fans around the globe can brew blends and single origins from the Crosby collection.

Jack and Mark have recently introduced a dedicated sustainability team and invested in new equipment to reduce waste and single-use packaging. They're also working with Liverpool John Moores University to run a full carbon-audit and offset the company's footprint.

ESTABLISHED
2014

ROASTER MAKE & SIZE
Toper 30kg
Toper 10kg
Ikawa Pro

OPEN
BY APPOINTMENT

COFFEE
COURSES

BEANS
AVAILABLE

ONLINE

www.crosbycoffee.co.uk   01515 385454
f @crosbycoffee   🐦 @crosbycoffeeltd   📷 @crosbycoffeeltd

32 NEIGHBOURHOOD COFFEE

Unit 22, Sandon Estate, Sandon Way, Liverpool, Merseyside, L5 9YN

For kid-in-a-sweet-shop vibes, discerning coffee fans head to Neighbourhood's online shop where they're greeted with a hefty selection of top-drawer speciality beans.

At any one time, the multi-award-winning roastery's webstore is stocked with up to 12 different coffees which range from cooperative lots to single-field micro batches. The team like to experiment with one-off processes, too, so coffees often make fleeting limited-edition appearances.

'THE TEAM LIKE TO EXPERIMENT WITH ONE-OFF PROCESSES'

Neighbourhood's sizeable collection has been made possible by its 2020 move to a roomier roastery and expansion of the roasting team. There's also a new, larger roaster on the way which will turn up the output another notch.

The team have worked hard to establish long-term partnerships with farming projects in Brazil, Colombia, Ethiopia and Guatemala and made several trips to origin to meet the farmers growing the goods.

ESTABLISHED
2014

ROASTER MAKE & SIZE
Giesen W15A
15kg

OPEN
BY APPOINTMENT

COFFEE
COURSES

BEANS
AVAILABLE
ONLINE   ONSITE

---

www.neighbourhoodcoffee.co.uk   01512 366741

f @neighbourhoodcoffee   🐦 @nhoodcoffee   📷 @neighbourhoodcoffee

33 DJANGO COFFEE CO.

Arch 94, Chadwick Court, Chadwick Street, Liverpool, Merseyside, L3 7EY

Roasting delicious coffee is paramount to the team at Django, but never at the expense of sustainability. Working with partners around the world, the roasting crew are uber conscientious about buying only the very best speciality beans which are ethically sourced and 100 per cent traceable.

Owner Ste Paweleck says: *'We believe sustainability is hugely important in the production of quality coffee. We want to minimise our carbon footprint and make sure each stage of the coffee chain, from harvesting to processing, is carried out with the kind of knowledge and understanding that does justice to everyone involved.'*

'PLANS ARE AFOOT FOR COURSES AND CUPPING EVENTS'

The team recently moved to larger premises in Liverpool and soon visitors will be able to get a close-up peek at the hand-roasting process. There are also plans afoot for the launch of courses and cupping events.

Inspiration for Django was initially sparked by Ste's travels through coffee-growing regions and his time spent in Melbourne's booming speciality scene. However, new adventures always beckon: this year's trips will include forging relationships with producers in Honduras, and a return to Guatemala.

ESTABLISHED
2016

ROASTER MAKE & SIZE
Giesen W6A 6kg

OPEN
BY APPOINTMENT

COFFEE
COURSES

BEANS
AVAILABLE

---

www.djangocoffeeco.com   01516 620354

f @djangocoffeeco   🐦 @djangocoffee   📷 @djangocoffeeco

North Wales

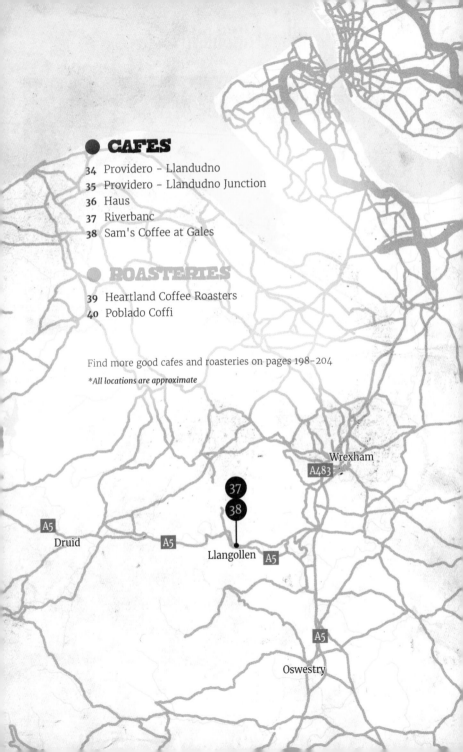

● CAFES

34 Providero – Llandudno
35 Providero – Llandudno Junction
36 Haus
37 Riverbanc
38 Sam's Coffee at Gales

● ROASTERIES

39 Heartland Coffee Roasters
40 Poblado Coffi

Find more good cafes and roasteries on pages 198–204

All locations are approximate

34 PROVIDERO – LLANDUDNO

112 Upper Mostyn Street, Llandudno, Conwy, Wales, LL30 2SW

L ike all cafes, this Llandudno stalwart has been through a testing 18 months. However, the much-loved meeting place has emerged bigger and better than ever.

In taking over the premises next door, Providero has now doubled in size and added a new studio, ProvSpace, which is home to a range of community events including dance and yoga classes. The Prov gang have also teamed up with a local bike shop to offer cycle hire and repair from the Mostyn Street hub. Even the retail selection has been given a makeover and now includes local, organic and eco-friendly products alongside a range of coffee paraphernalia.

 CHECK OUT THE CHALKBOARD FOR DEETS ON THE BEANS

While there have been lots of changes, the team's passion for speciality coffee has remained constant. Heartland Coffee (across town) roasts the house espresso and works closely with the Providero crew in the selection of single-estate beans for filter.

Similar care and attention goes into the food menu – the sourdough toasties and rainbow salad boxes are particularly special.

ESTABLISHED
2017

KEY ROASTER
Heartland
Coffee Roasters

BREWING METHOD
Espresso,
batch filter

MACHINE
Sanremo Opera

GRINDER
Mythos One
Clima Pro,
Mahlkonig EK43

OPENING HOURS
Mon–Sun
8.30am–4pm

 Gluten FREE

 BEANS AVAILABLE INSTORE

 WIFI

 CYCLE FRIENDLY

 OUTDOOR Seating

 DISABLED ACCESS

 BRING YOUR OWN Cup

DOG FRIENDLY

---

www.providero.co.uk   01492 338220

f @providero   🐦 @providero   📷 @providero.tea.coffee

35 PROVIDERO – LLANDUDNO JUNCTION

148 Conway Road, Llandudno Junction, Conwy, Wales, LL31 9DU

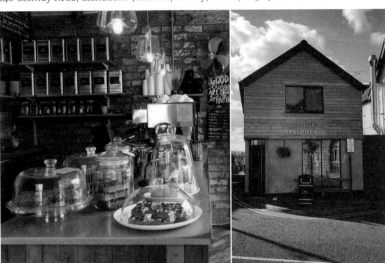

Those alighting at Llandudno Junction on the trail of adventures in Snowdonia don't have to travel far to get their first speciality coffee fix in North Wales.

Providero is just a short walk up the hill from the train station, and a friendly hub for locals and visitors who appreciate the art and craft of high-quality coffee. Beans from local roastery Heartland are prepared by a team of baristas who are passionate about brewing, and constantly refine their recipes in order to make each espresso and filter sing.

 CHECK OUT THE EVER-CHANGING DISPLAY OF LOCAL ARTWORK UPSTAIRS

The petite venue is affectionately known as Little Prov and is the sister to a roomier venue in Llandudno town. The Junction's compact home means there's only space for a teeny kitchen, but hungry travellers will still find a short and sweet inventory of sandwiches, pastries and cakes.

If you're self-catering nearby, stock up on local, organic and eco products – as well as a selection of coffee beans and brewing kit – from the newly extended retail selection.

ESTABLISHED
2014

KEY ROASTER
Heartland
Coffee Roasters

BREWING METHOD
Espresso,
batch filter

MACHINE
Sanremo Zoe

GRINDER
Mahlkonig EK43,
Mythos One
Clima Pro

OPENING HOURS
Mon-Sun
8am-2pm

 Gluten FREE

 BEANS AVAILABLE INSTORE

 WIFI

 CYCLE FRIENDLY

 DISABLED ACCESS

 BRING YOUR OWN Cup

 DOG FRIENDLY

www.providero.co.uk   01492 338220

f @providero   🐦 @providero   📷 @providero.tea.coffee

WAKE UP AND SMELL THE DAIRY-FREE COFFEE!

NO ADDED SUGAR

STRETCHES WITHOUT SPLITTING

DEVELOPED IN PARTNERSHIP WITH BARISTAS

MADE WITH ALMONDS GROWN ON OUR OWN FARMS

DESIGNED TO PERFECTLY COMPLEMENT ESPRESSO DRINKS

WWW.ALMONDBREEZE.CO.UK | @ALMONDBREEZEUK | @ALMONDBREEZEUK | INFO@ALMONDBREEZE.CO.UK

PRODUCT OF CALIFORNIA

36 HAUS

13 Penrhyn Road, Colwyn Bay, Colwyn, Wales, LL29 8LG

This independent cafe and bar on Colwyn Bay's Penrhyn Road blends German hospitality with Welsh creativity.

Proud Welsh chef Chris and German hospitality-pro Marita took over Haus in 2019. After just a year in business, the duo scooped a TripAdvisor Traveller's Choice award for their focus on quality ingredients, passion for all things coffee and inspiring brunch menu.

TRY THE 'FABULOUS BRIOCHE FRENCH TOAST' WITH CRISPY BACON AND MAPLE SYRUP

A straightforward drinks list concentrates on the art of espresso, which is crafted with beans roasted by Neighbourhood Coffee in Liverpool. There are also guest beans available as pourover and batch brew, plus artisan hot-drink alternatives from Brew Tea Co and Harry's Drinks Company.

The food offering is based on brunch, with dishes such as the Haus Full Breakfast (halloumi, bacon, free-range poached eggs, grilled tomato and smashed avo on toast) available to order all day. Those who like to go more off piste will find Haus specials such as harissa chicken with lemon couscous, broccoli, roasted sweet potato and toasted almonds.

ESTABLISHED
2019

KEY ROASTER
Neighbourhood Coffee

BREWING METHOD
Espresso, V60, batch brew

MACHINE
La Marzocco Linea PB

GRINDER
Fiorenzato F64 EVO

OPENING HOURS
Tue–Fri
8.30am–5pm
Sat
9am–3pm

www.hauscoffee.co.uk 01492 536610
f @hauscoffee @haus_coffee18

37 RIVERBANC

Bridge Street, Llangollen, Denbighshire, Wales, LL20 8PF

A n outdoor-adventure hub and hotel in rural North Wales isn't the first place you'd expect to find speciality coffee, but how else would visitors to this wild corner of the UK fuel their intrepid pursuits?

Riverbanc started out as an adventure company but when, in 2017, the team took over the Grade II-listed former Midland Bank building in the centre of Llangollen they had room to add accommodation and a cafe for weary adventurers in need of a recharge.

CHECK OUT THE WALLPAPER IN THE TOILETS. THAT'S ALL WE'RE GOING TO SAY

The building's spacious outdoor seating area overlooking the River Dee has always been a draw, but recent extension of the decking and the addition of covered seating has made the space a must-visit for year-round sipping. The quality coffee fuelling the buzzy chatter – outside and in – is roasted in Staffordshire by the team at Hasbean, and expertly fashioned into espresso drinks by Riverbanc's skilled baristas.

Cracking breakfast and brunch menus are on offer, too, and include the likes of homemade quiche with crunchy slaw.

ESTABLISHED
2018

KEY ROASTER
Hasbean

BREWING METHOD
Espresso

MACHINE
Nuova Simonelli
Aurelia T3

GRINDER
Mythos One

OPENING HOURS
Mon-Sun
8am-4pm

Gluten FREE

BEANS AVAILABLE INSTORE

WIFI

CYCLE FRIENDLY

OUTDOOR seating

DISABLED ACCESS

BRING YOUR OWN Cup

DOG FRIENDLY

www.riverbanc.co.uk   01978 799903

f @riverbanc   🐦 @riverbanc   📷 @riverbanc_llangollen

38 SAM'S COFFEE AT GALES

18 Bridge Street, Llangollen, Denbighshire, Wales, LL20 8PF

When Bold Street Coffee founder Sam Tawil moved from Liverpool to Llangollen with the aim of establishing a new coffee shop, two things were a given for the new venue: fantastic coffee and brunch with a disco beat.

At Gales' well-loved and long-established wine bar in the North Wales town, Sam's La Marzocco jostles with bottles of Malbec and Merlot for space at the bar, encapsulating the perpetual motion of daily (and nightly) life within the panelled walls.

LINGER LONGER BY BOOKING A NIGHT IN ONE OF GALES' GUEST ROOMS

There's always a single-origin espresso on the go, usually from Hasbean, alongside regularly switched-up guest filter options served via Chemex or pourover.

The breakfasts are legendary with cyclists and dog walkers who swing by for coffee and end up staying for the works. Even well-behaved pooches can nab themselves a sausage.

However, come Sunday it's all about catching up with friends over a deliciously lazy brunch – frequently served with tunes – either inside or in the Wine Garden. Those who prefer to wander will find themselves on the pretty banks of the River Dee before they've even taken the first sip of their takeaway flat white.

ESTABLISHED
2019

KEY ROASTER
Hasbean

BREWING METHOD
Espresso,
pourover, Chemex

MACHINE
La Marzocco
Linea PB

GRINDER
Mythos One,
Mazzer Robur E,
Mahlkonig Tanzania

OPENING HOURS
Mon-Sun
8am-2pm

 Gluten FREE

 BEANS AVAILABLE

 INSTORE

 WIFI

 CYCLE FRIENDLY

 OUTDOOR SEATING

 DISABLED ACCESS

 BRING YOUR OWN CUP

 COFFEE COURSES

 DOG FRIENDLY

www.gales.wine   01978 860089

f @samscoffeellangollen   @samscoffee_gales

Roasteries

North Wales

39 HEARTLAND COFFEE ROASTERS

Unit 6, Cwrt Roger Mostyn, Builder Street, Llandudno, North Wales, LL30 1DS

The team at this family-run roastery at the tip of North Wales take great care in sourcing their ever-shifting collection of speciality beans.

They've worked with importers DRWakefield since 2012, but more recently have also established direct-trade relationships with smallholders across the world. For example, Heartland was the first UK roastery to work with Caparao Speciality, through which it sources exciting Brazilian anaerobic-fermentation lots.

ESTABLISHED
2012

ROASTER MAKE & SIZE
Coffee-Tech
Ghibli 45kg
Coffee-Tech
Ghibli 15kg

CAFE ONSITE

OPEN BY APPOINTMENT

BEANS AVAILABLE

'SINK AN ESPRESSO AND CHAT COFFEE AT THE ROASTERY BREW BAR'

The two Coffee-Tech Ghibli roasters are fired up a number of times a week to bronze the broad selection of Heartland's single origins and blends. The team have been working on a new house blend to accompany the long-time favourite Landmark – a mix of South American and African lots which delivers the comforting cocoa notes of a banging espresso with a welcome dash of sweet, soft orange.

A fresh website has also been in development, allowing fans to order the latest Heartland coffees for delivery to their doors. If you're in the area you can pick up beans, sink an espresso and chat coffee with the team at the roastery brew bar.

www.heartland.coffee 01492 878757
f @heartlandcoffeeuk 🐦 @heartlandcoffi 📷 @heartland.coffee

40 POBLADO COFFI

Unit 1, Y Barics, Nantlle, Caernarfon, Gwynedd, Wales, LL54 6BD

If you're visiting Snowdonia or the beautiful North Wales coast, it's worth making a detour to this coffee roastery housed in a former quarrymen's barracks.

Every Saturday morning, founder Steffan Huws extends an open invitation to anyone who wishes to join the Poblado Plodders as they leave for a communal run around the old quarry, which ends with a brew and a chat back at the roastery. In summer, the barracks' doors stay open and locals and visiting coffee fans gather in the courtyard for open-air sipping and cake.

'IF THE DOOR IS OPEN, THE COFFEE MACHINE IS ON'

While the summer weekend sessions are the most popular, Steffan and team welcome roaming coffee folk for a chat and a brew any day of the week – if the door is open, the coffee machine is on.

At the heart of the roastery is a 15kg Giesen which roasts Poblado's curated collection of blends and single origins. Steffan is passionate about forging long-term relationships with growers, and the lots he sources from the Americas, Africa and Asia are selected for their sustainable credentials.

Signing up for one of the variety-pack subscriptions is the best way to sample the range of different beans – sippers can get the low-down on each of the coffees via the Poblado website.

ESTABLISHED
2013

ROASTER MAKE & SIZE
Giesen 15kg

CAFE ONSITE

OPEN TO THE PUBLIC

COFFEE COURSES

BEANS AVAILABLE

---

www.pobladocoffi.co.uk   01286 882555

f @pobladocoffi   🐦 @pobladocoffi   📷 @poblado_coffi

Greater
Manchester
& Cheshire

● CAFES

41 Grind & Tamp
42 Weaver and Wilde
43 Grindsmith Coffee Roasters
51 Propeller Coffee
52 Two Brothers – Altrincham
53 Two Brothers – Warrington
54 Little Yellow Pig
55 SHORT + STOUT
56 Jaunty Goat Coffee – Northgate Street
57 Bean & Cole
58 Jaunty Goat Coffee – Bridge Street

● ROASTERIES

59 Salford Roasters
61 Kickback Coffee
62 Two Brothers
63 Jaunty Goat

Find more good cafes and roasteries on pages 198–204

All locations are approximate

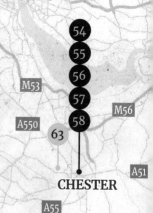

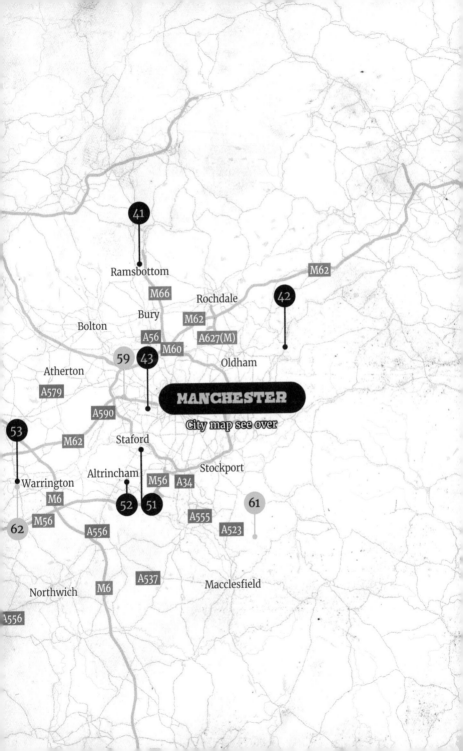

MANCHESTER

CENTRAL RETAIL DISTRICT

CAFES

44 Hampton & Voúis
45 200 Degrees
46 Atkinsons The Mackie Mayor
47 Ancoats Coffee Co. – Royal Mills
48 Fig + Sparrow
49 Takk Coffee House and Brunch Kitchen
50 Ancoats Coffee Co. – 111 Piccadilly

ROASTERIES

60 Ancoats Coffee Co.

Find more good cafes and roasteries on pages 198–204
All locations are approximate

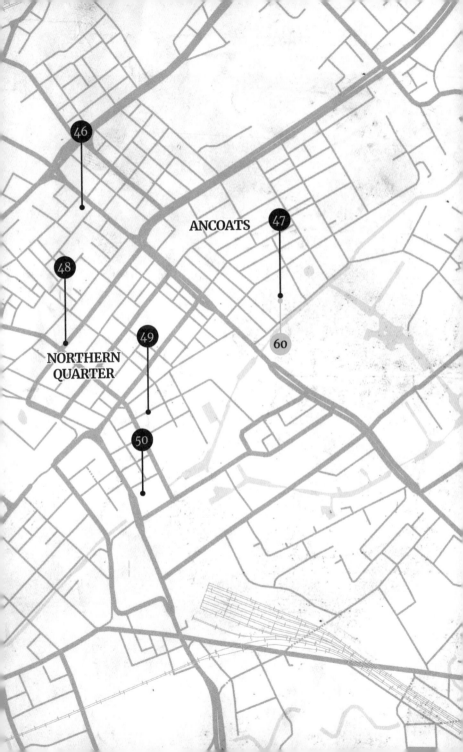

ANCOATS

NORTHERN
QUARTER

41 GRIND & TAMP

45 Bridge Street, Ramsbottom, Bury, Greater Manchester, BL0 9AD

This market-town coffee shop puts to bed any notion that you have to head into the city to find god-tier coffee in Greater Manchester.

Since 2016, the Grind & Tamp team of coffee enthusiasts have brought some of the UK's best beans to Ramsbottom. Revolution, Square Mile and Atkinsons are the current suppliers; however, the G&T crew like to mix things up so visit with an open mind and let the barista's recommendations guide you through the latest selection.

CHECK SOCIAL FOR THE LOW-DOWN ON UPCOMING SUPPER CLUBS

Every cup is expertly prepared with the kind of care and precision you'd expect at one of the Northern Quarter's next-level brew bars. Choose between espresso, V60, AeroPress and Chemex prep methods, then perch at the window bar as you explore the nuanced flavours.

The food menu is as progressive as its coffee counterpart, so it's worth scheduling a visit around breakfast or lunch in order to partake in the all-day brunch fest. If you've no time to linger, grab a golden-crusted pastel de nata with your coffee to-go.

ESTABLISHED
2016

KEY ROASTER
Revolution Coffee Roasters

BREWING METHOD
Espresso, V60, Chemex, AeroPress

MACHINE
Sanremo Café Racer

GRINDER
Mythos One, Mahlkonig K30, DIP DK-30

OPENING HOURS
Mon-Fri
7.30am-5pm
Sat
8.30am-4pm
Sun
10am-3pm

 Gluten FREE

 BEANS AVAILABLE INSTORE

 WIFI

 CYCLE FRIENDLY

 BRING YOUR OWN Cup

 COFFEE COURSES

 DOG FRIENDLY

www.grindandtampcoffee.uk   01706 558030

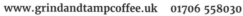 @grindandtampcoffee   @grind_tamp   @grind_tamp

42 WEAVER AND WILDE

30 High Street, Uppermill, Oldham, Greater Manchester, OL3 6HR

You'll leave this delicious find grasping more than just a full takeaway cup: the speciality coffee shop not only serves smashing brews and tempting seasonal dishes, it's also the local grocer and homewares emporium.

Farm-fresh veg, Saddleworth honey, Roger's Bakery bread and McLintock's Dairy milk are among the goodies fighting for shelf space with arty prints, houseplants and ceramic pots. Prepare for the inevitable by visiting armed with a stash of empty Tupperware tubs and tote bags.

 TREAT YOUR POOCH TO A SAUSAGE FROM THE DOGGY MENU

Before commencing an extensive browsing and feasting session, we'd recommend revving up with a flat white that stars the house blend Deer Hill from Dark Woods. Feeling adventurous? Plump for a guest filter.

The last year has seen the gastronomic treasure-trove partner more closely with local growers and producers, expand its seasonal menus and introduce natural wines to the boozy line-up. Head over Thursday to Saturday for sundown sipping – local beers and spirits feature, too – and an evening grazing menu.

ESTABLISHED
2019

KEY ROASTER
Dark Woods Coffee

BREWING METHOD
Espresso, batch filter

MACHINE
La Marzocco Linea PB

GRINDER
Anfim Pratica

OPENING HOURS
Mon-Wed
7.30am-5pm
Thu-Fri
7.30am-9pm
Sat
8am-9pm
Sun
8am-5pm

 Gluten FREE

 BEANS AVAILABLE INSTORE

 WIFI

 OUTDOOR SEATING

 BRING YOUR OWN CUP

 DOG FRIENDLY

www.weaverandwilde.co.uk 01457 878222

f @weaverandwilde @weaver_and_wilde

43 GRINDSMITH COFFEE ROASTERS

Unit 5-6, The Garage, MediaCity, Salford, Greater Manchester, M50 2BS

Grindsmith Coffee Roasters designed its Salford cafe with the goal of expertly fuelling the community that work and live in the area.

The venue caters brilliantly for MediaCity's worker bees and provides kickstart caffeine with a side of comfort, style and ambience. Urban concrete interiors are embellished by a beautiful stained-glass window, giant circular chandeliers, a bespoke geometric bar and cosy mezzanine level.

GUT INSTINCT DELIVERS THE GOODS FOR THE HOUSE OAT-MILK

Grindsmith is just as suitable for casual brunching and post-dog-walk relaxing as it is for an email blitz (FYI, the wifi is good and you won't feel out of place on your laptop). Food options range from hearty to nibbly – we recommend the stack of fluffy pancakes topped with berries.

The team serve top-notch espresso made from beans sourced from the three major coffee-growing regions, which are own-roasted just a few miles away in Ancoats. Visitors can choose between the house blend and a selection of seasonal single origins.

ESTABLISHED
2010

KEY ROASTER
Grindsmith
Coffee Roasters

BREWING METHOD
Espresso

MACHINE
Victoria Arduino
Black Eagle

GRINDER
Mythos One x 2,
Mahlkonig EK43

OPENING HOURS
Mon-Fri
8am-4pm
Sat-Sun
9am-4pm

 Gluten FREE

 BEANS AVAILABLE INSTORE

WIFI

 DISABLED ACCESS

 DOG FRIENDLY

www.grindsmith.com   07495 850032

f @grindsmith   🐦 @grindsmiths   📷 @grindsmithcoffee

44 HAMPTON & VOÚIS

31 Princess Street, Manchester, M2 4EW

Brunch in style at this Manchester cafe where the coffee and food are in the same league as the uber-glam interiors. A sleek Sanremo Café Racer machine perches on a polished concrete bar, while funky geometric fittings and natural light bouncing off white walls exude elegant simplicity.

Sink into a plush velvet chair and relish notes of hazelnut, chocolate and citrus in the popular Buxton house roast, which the H&V team created in collaboration with the Derbyshire roastery. Its blend of Brazilian, Thai and Ethiopian beans is delicious savoured alone, but even better paired with something divine from the food menu.

 THE COFFEE SYRUPS ARE ALL MADE IN-HOUSE, NATURAL AND FREE OF ANY NASTIES

From the outset, owners Nicky Hampton and Niko Voúis have been determined to ensure their food offering is as high-end as the chic interior styling, so the flexitarian menu – focused on Mediterranean cuisine – utilises fresh, unprocessed and local ingredients.

Follow açaí bowls, brunch dishes and grilled sandwiches with a slice of one of the decadent cakes or even a pile of vegan pancakes. The Biscoff and Bueno Stack, lavished in Lotus biscuit and caramel sauces, Lotus biscuit crumble and vanilla ice cream, is a voluptuous thrill.

ESTABLISHED
2018

KEY ROASTER
Buxton Coffee Roasters

BREWING METHOD
Espresso, V60, AeroPress

MACHINE
Sanremo Café Racer

GRINDER
Sanremo

OPENING HOURS
Mon-Fri
8am-4pm
Sat
9am-5pm
Sun
10am-4.30pm

 Gluten FREE

 BEANS AVAILABLE INSTORE

 WIFI

 BRING YOUR OWN Cup

 DOG FRIENDLY

www.hamptonandvouis.co.uk

f @hamptonandvouis @hamptonvouis

45 200 DEGREES

75 Mosley Street, Manchester, M2 3HR

Stepping into this 200 Degrees outpost is like sliding into a silky ristretto: the rich decor that envelops visitors is a prelude to the full-immersion coffee experience that awaits.

Freshly prepped dishes and bakes (including a good vegan offering) are served throughout the day to supplement the core pleasure of savouring 200 Degrees coffee (named after the slightly lower than usual temperature at which its beans are roasted) in its natural environment.

 CHECK OUT THE RETIRED 30KG ROASTER AT THE ENTRANCE

The roasting team source Rainforest Alliance-certified coffees and also support smaller uncertified farms that are committed to looking after workers, community and their local environment. The beans are then bronzed at the company's roastery in Nottingham.

This Mosley Street cafe also hosts a barista school (kitted out with four Victoria Arduino Primas), which gives an idea of the calibre of coffee prep you can expect here. Whether you're dashing through and grabbing a flattie to-go or sitting in to sip and savour, your coffee will always be expertly brewed and served.

ESTABLISHED
2021

KEY ROASTER
200 Degrees
Coffee Roasters

BREWING METHOD
Espresso, V60,
AeroPress

MACHINE
Victoria Arduino
Black Eagle

GRINDER
Mythos 2

OPENING HOURS
Mon-Fri
8.30am-5.30pm
Sat
9am-6pm
Sun
10am-6pm

 Gluten FREE

 BEANS AVAILABLE INSTORE

 WIFI

 OUTDOOR SEATING

 DISABLED ACCESS

 BRING YOUR OWN Cup.

COFFEE COURSES

www.200degs.com   01612 368620

f @200degs   🐦 @200degs   📷 @200degs

46 ATKINSONS THE MACKIE MAYOR

1 Eagle Street, Manchester, M4 5BU

Since 1837, Atkinsons has been a name synonymous with coffee in the North West. Lancaster is the roastery's native home (and where it has a handful of cafes), but you can also enjoy its caffeinated (and decaffeinated) magic at Mackie Mayor in the heart of Manchester's vibrant Northern Quarter.

One of a clutch of artisan traders in the Mackie Mayor food hall, Atkinsons is the worthy hub of all things coffee related. Here, the baristas showcase the full Atkinsons offering, and even roast beans on-site in a restored 100-year-old vintage Uno roaster.

 KICKSTART AN EVENING WITH A COFFEE- OR TEA-INFUSED COCKTAIL

The ever-evolving seasonal coffee menu includes a couple of espresso roasts: Atkinsons' Stereotype for milk-based coffee drinks and the fruitier Prototype which is best served black. There are also several adventurous single origins served on Clever Dripper. Whatever you choose, a wedge of cake from Atkinsons' Lancaster bakery is the natural accompaniment.

Get the Atkinsons experience with chums in the main Mackie seating area, take a brew to go, or recreate the vibe at home by grabbing a bag of beans (and the kit to buff up your barista skills) from the retail selection.

ESTABLISHED
2017

KEY ROASTER
Atkinsons
Coffee Roasters

BREWING METHOD
Espresso,
Clever Dripper

MACHINE
Sanremo Opera

GRINDER
Mythos One
Clima Pro,
Mahlkonig EK43

OPENING HOURS
Tue-Thu
9am-10pm
Fri-Sat
9am-11pm
Sun
9am-6pm

Gluten FREE

BEANS AVAILABLE
INSTORE

WIFI

CYCLE
FRIENDLY

OUTDOOR seating

DISABLED
ACCESS

BRING
YOUR OWN
Cup.

DOG
FRIENDLY

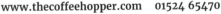

www.thecoffeehopper.com 01524 65470
f @atkinsonscoffeemackiemayor 🐦 @coffeehopper 📷 @atkinsonsatmackie

47 ANCOATS COFFEE CO. – ROYAL MILLS

Unit 9, Royal Mills, 17 Redhill Street, Manchester, M4 5BA

The team at Ancoats Coffee Co. have been roasting and serving coffee in the industrial heart of Manchester since 2013, establishing a loyal fanbase of wholesale and cafe customers.

Coffee tourists exploring the city will encounter Ancoats beans at speciality venues across the Northern Quarter and beyond, but the best place to sample them is at the source. Here at the Royal Mills HQ – a former cotton mill – visitors can savour the latest lots while surrounded by a background soundtrack of cafe clatter woven with the gentle chug of the Giesen roaster.

 CAFFEINE JITTERS? ORDER ONE OF THE KNOCKOUT CHEESE TOASTIES

There's an impressive selection of coffees to choose from and it changes seasonally to reflect the global bean harvests. Newbies should start with the Warehouse City espresso blend, before exploring the high-end single-origin offerings. Founder Jamie Boland likes to work with beans from unusual origins such as Myanmar and Uganda, so expect to be surprised and delighted by new finds.

The authentically industrial cafe (think bare-brick walls, steel columns and arched windows) doesn't just attract coffee aficionados: it's also a popular hangout for touring musicians, bands and DJs.

ESTABLISHED
2013

KEY ROASTER
Ancoats Coffee Co.

BREWING METHOD
Espresso, V60, AeroPress, batch brew, Chemex, cold brew

MACHINE
Victoria Arduino VA388 Black Eagle

GRINDER
Mythos One, Mythos 2, Mahlkonig EK43

OPENING HOURS
Mon–Fri
8am–6pm
Sat
9am–6pm
Sun
10am–5pm

 Gluten FREE

 BEANS AVAILABLE INSTORE

 WIFI

 CYCLE FRIENDLY

 OUTDOOR seating

 DISABLED ACCESS

 BRING YOUR OWN Cup

 COFFEE COURSES

DOG FRIENDLY

www.ancoats-coffee.co.uk   01612 368494

f @ancoatscoffeeco   🐦 @ancoatscoffeeco   @ @ancoatscoffeeco

48 FIG + SPARROW

20 Oldham Street, Northern Quarter, Manchester, M1 1JN

This design-led coffee shop has resided in the heart of the Northern Quarter for almost a decade, becoming a well-loved pit stop for a dose of great coffee, delicious food and friendly faces.

Sisters Laura and Hannah took the Fig + Sparrow reins from founders Jan and Emily Dixon in 2020 and have made small tweaks to turn it into their own dream cafe. Most notably, they've installed a new kitchen which has enabled them to extend the brunch and lunch menus.

Insider's Tip — MAKE AN AFTERNOON VISIT FOR CRAFT BEERS AND WINES BY THE GLASS

They've also freshened up the coffee offering, enlisting local roastery Grindsmith who have masterminded a bespoke Fig + Sparrow house blend called Sierra. It's a cracking all-rounder that tastes just as good black as it does paired with silky steamed milk.

Plonk yourself on a window seat with your filter coffee and slice of something homemade (the fig rolls are, naturally, a speciality) to observe the busy goings on on Oldham Street, or venture further inside and cosy up with a flat white in one of the booths. There's also a handful of outside seats for sipping in the Manchester sunshine.

ESTABLISHED
2013

KEY ROASTER
Grindsmith Coffee Roasters

BREWING METHOD
Espresso, AeroPress, V60, Chemex

MACHINE
La Marzocco Linea PB

GRINDER
Victoria Arduino Mythos One, Mahlkonig EK43

OPENING HOURS
Mon-Fri
9am-5pm
Sat
9am-6pm
Sat-Sun
10am-5pm

 Gluten FREE

 BEANS AVAILABLE INSTORE

 WIFI

 CYCLE FRIENDLY

 OUTDOOR seating

 DISABLED ACCESS

 BRING YOUR OWN Cup

 DOG FRIENDLY

www.figandsparrow.co.uk   07866 553369

f @figsparrow   🐦 @figsparrow   📷 @figsparrow

49 TAKK COFFEE HOUSE AND BRUNCH KITCHEN

6 Tariff Street, Northern Quarter, Manchester, M1 2FF

A couple of blocks from Manchester's Piccadilly Train Station, Takk Coffee House and Brunch Kitchen pays homage to Scandinavian and Icelandic cafe culture.

Since it opened in 2013, Takk has been one of the most reliable spots in the city for excellent coffee and food. Brunch has always been its strong point, and locals flood into the Scandi-chic space to feast on staples such as guacamole on sourdough and 'nduja eggs.

 FOR THE ULTIMATE COFFEE EXPERIENCE, ASK TO SEE THE EXCLUSIVE CRYO-MENU

In 2021, the Tariff Street venue joined the Grindsmith family, further cementing the roastery's association with the finest coffee in Manchester. The partnership has enabled the Takk team to take roasting in-house and refine a selection of excellent single-origin espressos, including the crowd-pleasing Finca Miravalle from El Salvador.

The coffees served from the stunning new brew bar (created by iconic Manchester designer Tim Denton) change on a weekly basis to showcase the team's latest roasts alongside guests from the best of the UK and European roasting scene. The baristas are skilled in a multitude of brewing methods and can pair your pick of the beans to the serve style that'll best show them off.

ESTABLISHED
2013

KEY ROASTER
Takk:
Northern Projekt

BREWING METHOD
Espresso, V60,
AeroPress, batch
brew, cold brew

MACHINE
Modbar

GRINDER
Mythos One
Clima Pro

OPENING HOURS
Mon-Fri
9am-4pm
Sat-Sun
10am-4pm

 Gluten FREE

 BEANS AVAILABLE INSTORE

 WIFI

 CYCLE FRIENDLY

 OUTDOOR seating

 BRING YOUR OWN Cup

 DOG FRIENDLY

www.takkmcr.com   07948 806588

f @takkmcr   🐦 @takkmcr   @takkmcr

50 ANCOATS COFFEE CO. – 111 PICCADILLY

111 Piccadilly, London Road, Manchester, M1 2HY

After eight years of roasting and serving coffee at the Royal Mills roastery-cafe HQ, June 2021 saw the launch of Ancoats Coffee Co.'s new sister venue in the heart of the city.

The new digs are to be found on the ground floor of the freshly refurbished and super sustainable (it's WELL certified) 111 Piccadilly building. Just a short dash from Piccadilly Train Station, it's the perfect spot for much-needed post-commute caffeination. It's also a good call for an early evening party-starter thanks to the talented baristas shaking Espresso Martinis till 6pm.

 ### THERE'S LOTS OF SPACE, SO DON'T BE SHY ABOUT LAUNCHING YOUR LAPTOP AND HANGING OUT

The coffee menu at 111 mirrors that at HQ, with fresh batches from the roastery arriving daily. Crowd-pleasing house espresso Warehouse City is joined by a collection of rare and interesting single origins including Santa Isabel: Ancoats' first biodynamic coffee which was directly sourced in Guatemala by founder Jamie Boland.

Friendly, knowledgeable baristas are happy to talk through the day's offerings which can be prepared as espresso, batch filter and cold brew. Take a trip across town and visit the Royal Mills site to experience an extended selection of brew methods.

ESTABLISHED
2021

KEY ROASTER
Ancoats
Coffee Co.

BREWING METHOD
Espresso, batch
brew, cold brew

MACHINE
Victoria Arduino
Eagle One

GRINDER
Mythos One,
Mythos 2,
Mahlkonig EK43

OPENING HOURS
Mon-Fri
8am-6pm

Gluten
FREE

BEANS
AVAILABLE
INSTORE

WIFI

CYCLE
FRIENDLY

OUTDOOR
seating

DISABLED
& ACCESS

BRING
YOUR OWN
cup

DOG
FRIENDLY

---

www.ancoats-coffee.co.uk   01612 368494

f @ancoatscoffeeco   🐦 @ancoatscoffeeco   📷 @ancoatscoffeeco

51 PROPELLER COFFEE

7 Northenden Road, Sale, Greater Manchester, M33 2DH

Propeller, on Sale's Northenden Road, is the kind of friendly neighbourhood coffee shop most of us can only dream of having close to home.

Its most obvious charm is the cracking house espresso, which founder Benny Au masterminded with the team at Cartwheel Coffee in Nottingham. A 70/30 blend of Brazilian/Ethiopian beans, it tastes sensational when prepared as the house-favourite flat white. There's also a guest roast (switched up every two months) from the likes of UE Coffee Roasters and Heart and Graft.

HOMEMADE COLD-DRIP COFFEE IS A REFRESHING CHOICE IN SUMMER

The cafe's food offering comes in a close second to the brews and is the kind of familiar fodder we all crave but can't always be faffed to whip up at home. Think plump poachies on avocado toast, toasted waffles showered in berries, and crisp golden pastries (the latter made by Pot Kettle Black Bakehouse).

The cafe's other attractive quality is the service: the team are super helpful and the entire experience is family friendly, building coffee aficionados of the future – one babyccino at a time.

ESTABLISHED
2018

KEY ROASTER
Cartwheel
Coffee Roasters

BREWING METHOD
Espresso,
batch filter, drip

MACHINE
Sanremo
Verona RS

GRINDER
Mahlkonig EK43,
Victoria Arduino
Mythos One,
Mahlkonig E65S
GbW

OPENING HOURS
Mon-Fri
8am-4pm
Sat-Sun
9.30am-3.30pm

 BEANS AVAILABLE INSTORE

 WIFI

 CYCLE FRIENDLY

 OUTDOOR SEATING

 BRING YOUR OWN Cup

 DOG FRIENDLY

01619 693560

f @propellercoffeeuk @propellercoffee_sale

52 TWO BROTHERS COFFEE – ALTRINCHAM

53 Stamford New Road, Altrincham, Cheshire, WA14 1DS

This Altrincham indie has rapidly expanded since it opened in 2017: two sister venues (the first in Warrington, the second in St Helens) and a roastery have been added to the family.

While the business has blossomed, founders (and brothers) Steve and Dave's drive to create great coffee to be shared with friends remains exactly the same. However now, thanks to the launch of their own roastery, the duo have full control of the beans they brew.

 HEAD TO THE TWO BROTHERS WEBSITE FOR HOME-BREWING TUTORIALS

The two grinders at this flagship cafe are stocked with the freshest finds from the Two Brothers roastery (based at the Warrington Market outpost). Head roaster Sean roasts seasonally, switching up the selection of single origins on offer every few months to reflect what tastes great.

The cafe's all-black interior and industrial lighting nod to Steve and Dave's previous careers in engineering and result in a cosy space in which to settle down with a flat white and something delish from the counter of traybakes.

ESTABLISHED
2017

KEY ROASTER
Two Brothers

BREWING METHOD
Espresso, V60, batch brew

MACHINE
Sanremo Opera

GRINDER
Mythos One, Mahlkonig EK43

OPENING HOURS
Mon–Fri
7am–5pm
Sat
8am–5pm
Sun
10am–4pm

INSTORE

WIFI

CYCLE
FRIENDLY

OUTDOOR
seating

DISABLED
ACCESS

BRING
YOUR OWN
cup.

DOG
FRIENDLY

www.twobrothers.coffee   01616 131821

f @twobrotherscoffeeltd   🐦 @2btwobrothers   📷 @twobrotherscoffee

53 TWO BROTHERS COFFEE – WARRINGTON

Warrington Market, 2 Time Square, Warrington, Cheshire, WA1 2NT

Warrington town centre was speciality sparse until the Two Brothers crew rocked up in 2020 to establish their second coffee shop (the first is down the M56 in Altrincham).

They took over a spot in the new state-of-the-art Warrington Market (a creative hub of over 50 indie traders) and started slinging first-rate espresso and brewing single-origin filters for coffee-loving locals and visitors.

EARLY RISER? CHECK OUT THE NEW BREAKFAST MENU

There's no missing 2B when you enter the market as the enticing waft of gently roasting coffee leads punters directly to the brew bar. When the team moved into the new digs, they also brought their micro roastery (which used to be in the basement of the Altrincham shop) in order to expand the range of own-roasted beans.

Make a trip to see what roaster Sean is crafting, then take a perch to sample the latest single origin on V60. If you like what you're sipping, you can even pick up a box of the same beans to brew at home.

ESTABLISHED
2020

KEY ROASTER
Two Brothers

BREWING METHOD
Espresso, V60, batch brew

MACHINE
La Marzocco FB80

GRINDER
Mythos One, Mahlkonig EK43

OPENING HOURS
Mon–Sun
9am–5pm
(second Sunday of the month only)

 Gluten FREE

 BEANS AVAILABLE INSTORE

 WIFI

 CYCLE FRIENDLY

 OUTDOOR seating

 DISABLED ACCESS

 BRING YOUR OWN Cup

www.twobrothers.coffee

f @twobrotherscoffeeltd 🐦 @2btwobrothers 📷 @twobrotherscoffee

54 LITTLE YELLOW PIG

31 Westminster Road, Hoole, Chester, Cheshire, CH2 3AX

Despite the difficulties of 2020, this little piggy opened a sister site in Nantwich last year, giving the people of Cheshire another laid-back spot in which to enjoy speciality-grade coffee and easy-going brunch dishes.

This, the original outpost in Hoole, has a relaxed neighbourhood vibe which makes customers instantly feel at ease. Its bright colour palette (you can't miss the smoky-blue exterior and, inside, the sunshine-yellow LYP mural) and genuine friendly welcome are guaranteed to coax a smile on even the dreariest Monday morning.

 CHASE BRUNCH WITH A HOMEMADE BAKE – THE RASPBERRY AND WHITE-CHOC BLONDIES ARE DELISH

Beans from Hundred House, Dark Arts and Red Bank (among other hero roasteries) give coffee fans something to grin about. The team at Hundred House in Shropshire roast a signature coffee for the La Marzocco machine, which the team recommend drinking as a silky flat white, while guests take turns on batch.

The food offering is a classic line-up of tried-and-tested brunch dishes and sourdough toasties. There are plenty of veggie and vegan options, too, including the Vegan Stuff on Sourdough which is a feast of avo, sundried tomatoes, mushrooms and spinach.

ESTABLISHED
2014

KEY ROASTER
Hundred
House Coffee

BREWING METHOD
Espresso,
batch brew

MACHINE
La Marzocco
Linea Classic

GRINDER
Mythos One x 2

OPENING HOURS
Mon-Sat
9am-5pm
Sun
10am-3pm

 Gluten FREE

BEANS AVAILABLE INSTORE

 WIFI

 OUTDOOR seating

 BRING YOUR OWN cup

 DOG FRIENDLY

www.littleyellowpig.co.uk   01244 637220
f @littleyellowpighoole   @littleyellowpig31

55 SHORT + STOUT

3a Ermine Road, Hoole, Chester, Cheshire, CH2 3PN

This corner coffee shop in Hoole is the kind of community hangout every coffee lover wishes they had at the end of their street.

It deals in the holy trinity of great coffee, delicious food and genuinely friendly service, so it's usually chocka with locals grabbing coffee on the way to work, and visitors who've made the trip to soak up the welcoming neighbourhood vibes while they dig into brunch.

 DON'T BE DETERRED IF IT LOOKS PACKED OUT; THERE'S ADDITIONAL SEATING HIDDEN AWAY DOWNSTAIRS

Make the short walk from the centre of Chester to savour Manchester-roasted beans from Ancoats and guest roasts prepared as espresso, cold brew and batch. Then pair your pick with Aussie-inspired dishes from the brunch menu, such as the rhubarb and custard pancake stack, and corn and zucchini fritters served with beetroot hummus, smashed avo and poached eggs.

If you've no time to stop for brekkie, brunch or lunch, you can still indulge in SHORT + STOUT's homemade spoils: pick up a box of cakes with your coffee to-go and take some incredible edibles away with you.

ESTABLISHED
2018

KEY ROASTER
Ancoats Coffee Co.

BREWING METHOD
Espresso,
cold brew,
batch brew

MACHINE
La Marzocco
Linea PB

GRINDER
Mythos One Clima
Pro, Mazzer Mini

OPENING HOURS
Mon-Fri
8am-4pm
Sat
9am-4pm
Sun
10am-2pm

 Gluten FREE

   BEANS AVAILABLE / INSTORE

WIFI

CYCLE FRIENDLY

OUTDOOR seating

 BRING YOUR OWN Cup.

 DOG FRIENDLY

01244 343378

f @SHORT + STOUT   🐦 @shortandstout_   📷 @shortandstoutltd

56 JAUNTY GOAT COFFEE – NORTHGATE STREET

128 Northgate Street, Chester, Cheshire, CH1 2HT

The launch of Chester's first plant-based coffee shop saw the highly anticipated expansion of the Jaunty Goat herd. This, the second member of the crew, shares the characteristic Scandi style of the Bridge Street site and is all chunky wood and sleek industrial styling softened by lush indoor foliage.

The Jaunty team showcase ethically produced coffee alongside a deliciously diverse vegan menu which promises to please even the most devoted omnivore.

 GRAB A BAG OF OWN-ROASTED JAUNTY GOAT BEANS TO BREW AT HOME

Planet-friendly and gluten-free brunch classics are served alongside carbon-neutral house espresso and filter roasts. An array of loose-leaf teas and cold drinks also features. The coffee beans are consciously sourced before being roasted at the Goat's own roastery in the city, while baked goodies are delivered daily from the new JG bakery.

Dogs are welcome and bike racks are available, so the whole family can take a moment to savour the sunshine on the seating outside – or marvel at the talents of the friendly baristas at work within.

ESTABLISHED
2019

KEY ROASTER
Jaunty Goat Coffee

BREWING METHOD
Espresso,
AeroPress,
V60, Chemex,
cold brew

MACHINE
Victoria Arduino
Eagle One

GRINDER
Mythos One,
Mahlkonig EK43

OPENING HOURS
Mon–Sun
9am–5pm

 Gluten FREE

 BEANS AVAILABLE INSTORE

 WIFI

 CYCLE FRIENDLY

 OUTDOOR seating

 BRING YOUR OWN Cup.

 DOG FRIENDLY

www.jauntygoat.co.uk   01244 421492

f @jauntygoat   🐦 @jaunty_goat   📷 @jaunty_goat

57 BEAN & COLE

41 Frodsham Street, Chester, Cheshire, CH1 3JJ

This fiercely independent and award-winning Chester coffee shop specialises in serving mind-blowing beans from a huge roll call of UK roasters, so visitors get a palate-popping array of flavours to try, every time.

Beans from Curve, Round Hill, Origin, Quarter Horse, Dark Arts, Hard Lines and Ozone are just a few of the recent pickings. If the boggling line-up has you all of a fluster, a good starting place is the single-origin house espresso from Assembly, which changes seasonally.

TUCK INTO LOCALLY CRAFTED BEAR BAKERY SOURDOUGH IN ONE OF THE TOAST-BASED DISHES

Those ready to branch out should ask for a recommendation as the team are keen to make coffee accessible for all and will happily give advice. It's this friendliness that makes Bean & Cole feel more like a neighbourhood cafe than its city-centre location might suggest.

The recent addition of the Moccamaster batch brewer has been a big hit, so consider opting for a juicy natural filter to accompany your freshly prepped sarnie, Kookaburra Bakehouse cake or brekkie bowl.

ESTABLISHED
2018

KEY ROASTER
Assembly Coffee

BREWING METHOD
Espresso,
batch brew

MACHINE
Victoria Arduino
White Eagle

GRINDER
Victoria Arduino
Mythos One x 2,
Mahlkonig EK43

OPENING HOURS
Mon-Sat
9am-5pm
Sun
10am-5pm

Gluten FREE

BEANS AVAILABLE
INSTORE

WIFI

CYCLE FRIENDLY

DISABLED ACCESS

BRING YOUR OWN Cup

DOG FRIENDLY

01244 639060
🐦 @beancolecoffee 📷 @beanandcolecoffee

58 JAUNTY GOAT COFFEE - BRIDGE STREET

57 Bridge Street, Chester, Cheshire, CH1 1NG

The he original Jaunty Goat's light-drenched and pared-back Scandi interior sets the tone for the cafe's plant-centric menu and sleek coffee craftsmanship.

Roasted at its own local roastery, Jaunty Goat's coffee (like its food) is sourced with sustainability at its heart. The cafe even has its own bakery just over the road, which helps keep food miles to a minimum.

VEG OUT WITH JAUNTY GOAT'S HEAVENLY VEGGIE EGGS BENNY

A jaunty menu offers a myriad of vegetarian and vegan dishes, from house granola to orecchiette pasta – and everything in between. It's all about the options here, so customers can size-up the salad portions, size-down dishes to suit kids' appetites, and choose from the full spectrum of milk alternatives.

While the food's really good, it's coffee that puts a spring in the step of the Jaunty Goat team so, when you visit, make the most of their expertise and get the low-down on the source and science behind your brew.

ESTABLISHED
2015

KEY ROASTER
Jaunty Goat Coffee

BREWING METHOD
Espresso, AeroPress, V60, Chemex, cold brew

MACHINE
Sanremo Opera 2.0

GRINDER
Mythos One, Mythos 2, Mahlkonig EK43

OPENING HOURS
Mon-Sat
8am-6pm
Sun
9am-6pm

Gluten FREE

BEANS AVAILABLE
INSTORE

WIFI

CYCLE FRIENDLY

OUTDOOR seating

DISABLED ACCESS

BRING YOUR OWN Cup

DOG FRIENDLY

www.jauntygoat.co.uk   01244 421492

f @jauntygoat   🐦 @jaunty_goat   📷 @jaunty_goat

Roasteries

Greater Manchester & Cheshire

59 SALFORD ROASTERS

Unit E, Protector Lamp Business Park, Salford, Greater Manchester, M30 9PH

During the madness of 2020, the Salford Roasters tribe took the plunge and upped sticks to new premises, providing a bigger base for their banging beans, top-notch team and focus on social value.

The gang have developed four blends to encourage those new to speciality but the focus of the roasting operation is definitely on single origins. The reason? To shine a spotlight on the talent of the producers: *'Single-origin coffees portray the hard work that goes on at farm level to produce the quality in the cup, and we know the story behind the individual coffees is important to our online customers,'* says founder Nik Storey.

'SINGLE-ORIGIN COFFEES PORTRAY THE HARD WORK THAT GOES ON AT FARM LEVEL'

Beans from Africa and Central America are bronzed on an Italian smokeless air roaster. House favourites include the much-loved Signature Blend and Nik's 'find of 2020': Bukonzo Dream, a Ugandan lot featuring strawberry and peach notes with a stunning tropical-fruit finish.

The crew are keen to make quality coffee all-inclusive, so rookie sippers and experienced connoisseurs are all welcome at the on-site espresso bar or to take a roastery tour and dive into the Salford speciality experience.

ESTABLISHED
2016

ROASTER MAKE & SIZE
IMF 15kg

CAFE ONSITE

OPEN TO THE PUBLIC

COFFEE COURSES

BEANS AVAILABLE

---

www.salfordroasters.co.uk   07786 382000
f @salfordroasters   🐦 @salfordroasters   ⃝ @salfordroasters

60 ANCOATS COFFEE CO.

Unit 9, Royal Mills, 17 Redhill Street, Manchester, M4 5BA

After spending eight years refining their roast style, the team at this Manchester roastery have recently turned their attention to sourcing.

While they've always worked with ethical specialist-import partners, a shift in focus to working directly with farmers and cooperatives has resulted in around 40 per cent of the Ancoats collection now being direct trade. One of the most exciting lots on the bill is Santa Isabel, Ancoats' first biodynamic coffee which owner and Q grader Jamie Boland discovered on a recent trip to Guatemala.

'FINDING THE SWEET SPOT TO HIGHLIGHT THE BRIGHT JUICY SIDE OF COFFEES'

Back at the roastery (a former cotton mill in Manchester's industrial heartland), Jamie and co adopt a flavour-forward roasting style which he describes as *'finding the sweet spot to highlight the bright, juicy side of coffees'*.

The Grade II-listed roastery's adjoining cafe and retail space enables coffee fans to sample the latest off-piste single origins, pick up bags of coffee to brew at home and sneak a peek at the Giesen roaster toasting the next batch. It's also a great place for celeb spotting: the building is often used as a location for films, TV shows and adverts.

ESTABLISHED
2013

ROASTER MAKE & SIZE
Giesen W6 6kg
Ikawa Pro50 50g

CAFE ONSITE

OPEN BY APPOINTMENT

COFFEE COURSES

BEANS AVAILABLE

www.ancoats-coffee.co.uk 01612 368494
 @ancoatscoffeeco @ancoatscoffeeco @ancoatscoffeeco

61 KICKBACK COFFEE

Unit 3, The Old Brickworks, Pott Shrigley, Cheshire, SK10 5RX

Given that Kickback Coffee founder Alex Shaw first got into the industry by attempting to roast beans from eBay in a secondhand popcorn machine, the company has come a long way.

The professional roastery-cafe was established in 2018 in Pott Shrigley and a second venue was launched in Altrincham shortly after. Both are open to the public, so visitors can savour a cup of fresh coffee while watching the next batch in the roaster.

ESTABLISHED
2018

ROASTER MAKE & SIZE
Giesen W15 15kg
Giesen W6 6kg

CAFE ONSITE

COFFEE COURSES

BEANS AVAILABLE

'SAVOUR A CUP OF FRESH COFFEE WHILE WATCHING THE NEXT BATCH IN THE ROASTER'

Alex and team import coffee from a wide range of countries, purchasing directly from farmers and through trusted importers. Head roaster Josh is a fount of speciality knowledge and roasts at the Altrincham venue on a Saturday, when visitors can pose any burning questions.

If you visit and aren't sure what to sample, the signature espresso blend is a great place to start. The balance of Nicaraguan, Colombian and Ethiopian bean's features nutty notes and raisin sweetness. It's accompanied by a solid selection of single origins which can also be sipped at the roastery-cafes or ordered via the Kickback website.

www.kickbackcoffee.co.uk   01625 409616
f @kickbackcoffeeuk   🖸 @kickbackcoffee

62 TWO BROTHERS

Warrington Market, 2 Time Square, Warrington, Cheshire, WA1 2NT

Two Brothers roastery started out as a micro operation in the basement of its Altrincham coffee shop. Such was the demand for its single-origin beans that, when the 2B team opened a second site in Warrington Market, they moved the roasting set-up into it.

With the move came a kit upgrade and the arrival of a shiny new 15kg Giesen roaster, which now takes centre stage at the roastery-cafe. Visitors can grab an espresso or filter coffee and watch the roasters get to work on the next batch of beans.

'TWO BROTHERS NOW WORKS WITH SOCIAL-ENTERPRISE FARMS'

The team take a seasonal approach and refresh the coffee offering on a quarterly basis. They're open to all origins and processes, trying a vast selection of samples from sourcing partners before picking three or four of their favourites to roll out across the three 2B coffee shops and online Coffee Club subscription service.

A new sourcing approach means Two Brothers now also works with social-enterprise farms, so schools, sustainable initiatives and community projects at origin are supported.

ESTABLISHED
2019

ROASTER MAKE & SIZE
Giesen W15 15kg
Aillio Bullet 1kg

---

www.twobrothers.coffee   07883 787530

f @twobrotherscoffeeltd   🐦 2btwobrothers   📷 @twobrotherscoffee

63 JAUNTY GOAT

Unit 46, CoWorkz, Minerva Avenue, Chester, Cheshire, CH1 4QL

Jaunty Goat is renowned for its commitment to the environment. Plant-based menus are at the heart of its coffee shops and, in 2020, the company took things a step further and established its own roastery to guarantee full traceability and sustainability from farm to filter.

Despite the team's insatiable appetite for tracking down new and interesting coffees, Jaunty Goat is unwavering in its commitment to only sourcing ethically. The current house espresso roast, for example, is from the Aquiares Estate – the first farm in Costa Rica to fulfil the requirements of the Rainforest Alliance Climate Module.

'JAUNTY GOAT IS UNWAVERING IN ITS COMMITMENT TO ONLY SOURCE ETHICALLY'

As well as safeguarding the planet through its coffee-sourcing practices, Jaunty Goat also does its utmost to minimise the impact that comes from its own activities.

All of the own-roasted coffee supplied to its Chester coffee shops and bakery, as well as to local wholesale clients, is delivered in reusable tubs to reduce the plastic packaging waste that would arise from single-use coffee bags.

ESTABLISHED
2020

ROASTER MAKE & SIZE
Probat
Probatone 12kg

BEANS AVAILABLE
ONLINE

---

www.jauntygoat.co.uk   01244 421492
f @jauntygoat   🐦 @jaunty_goat   📷 @jaunty_goat

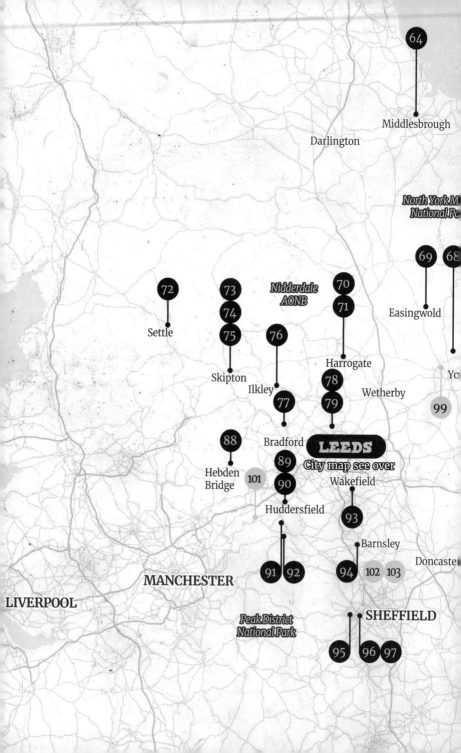

● CAFES

64 Off the Ground
65 Koda
66 Yay Coffee!
67 Two Gingers Coffee
68 The Curious Coffee Company – Haxby
69 The Curious Coffee Company – Easingwold
70 Bean & Bud
71 Starling Independent Bar Cafe Kitchen
72 Lay of the Land
73 Bean Loved
74 Steep & Filter
75 The Clubhouse Coffee & Cycles
76 Toast House
77 Tambourine Coffee
78 Fika North
79 Bowery
88 Squeeze Cafe & Deli
89 Coffeevolution
90 Arcade Coffee & Food
91 Wired Coffee and Cake
92 Bloc Cafe
93 KRA:FT Koffee
94 Old George Coffee House
95 The Whaletown Coffee Company
96 Albie's Coffee
97 Mow's Coffee

● ROASTERIES

98 Roost Coffee & Roastery
99 York Emporium
101 Dark Woods Coffee
102 Frazer's Coffee Roasters
103 Forge Coffee Roasters

Find more good cafes and roasteries on pages 198–204

All locations are approximate

65
66

North Riding
Forest Park

98

Scarborough

Malton

67

Hull

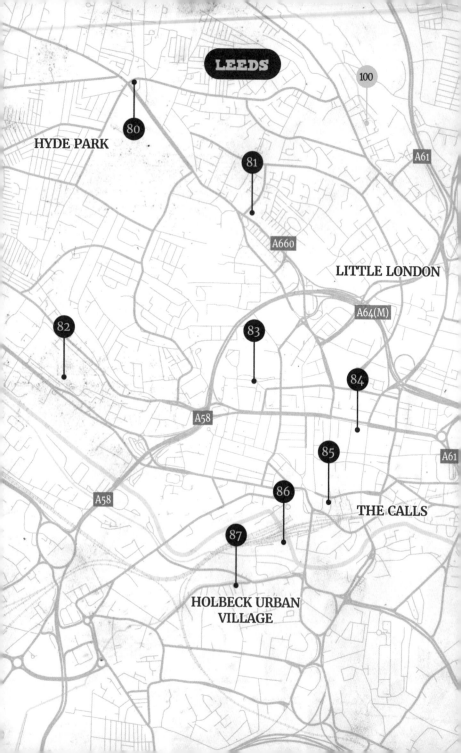

● CAFES

80 Coffee on the Crescent

81 Dot the Lions

82 Archive

83 Stage Espresso & Brew Bar

84 Kapow Coffee

85 Laynes Espresso

86 Out of the Woods – Granary Wharf

87 Out of the Woods – Water Lane

● ROASTERIES

100 Echelon Coffee Roasters

Find more good cafes and roasteries on pages 198–204

All locations are approximate

64 OFF THE GROUND

63 Grange Road, Middlesbrough, North Yorkshire, TS1 5AS

Despite navigating 18 months of lockdowns and restrictions, since the last edition of the *North, Midlands & North Wales Guide* the team at Off the Ground have taken their Middlesbrough hangout next level.

They kicked off the upgrades by installing a kitchen to broaden the cafe's range of delicious edibles and now everything, including the brioche buns, bagels and sourdough, is made in-house from scratch. Next up was the acquisition of an alcohol licence to extend opening hours on Fridays and Saturdays so patrons can explore the 100-strong craft beer offering.

 THE HOUSE-BRINED SALT-BEEF REUBEN SANDWICH IS A MUST TRY

A new outdoor seating area to the rear of the cafe has increased the number of regulars and newbies Off the Ground can squeeze in when the weather's good. It's also where the Friday night stone-baked pizza sessions take place in summer.

The coffee remains as great as ever and is roasted by speciality pioneer Origin in Cornwall. Two or three roasts are always on the agenda and visitors will almost certainly encounter a chocolatey, nut-forward single origin, alongside something funky such as a naturally processed African coffee.

ESTABLISHED
2017

KEY ROASTER
Origin Coffee Roasters

BREWING METHOD
Espresso, V60, AeroPress, batch brew

MACHINE
La Marzocco Linea PB

GRINDER
Victoria Arduino Mythos One x 2, Mahlkonig EK43

OPENING HOURS
Mon–Thu
10am–4pm
Fri–Sat
10am–11pm

BEANS AVAILABLE INSTORE

WIFI

CYCLE FRIENDLY

OUTDOOR SEATING

DISABLED ACCESS

BRING YOUR OWN Cup.

DOG FRIENDLY

www.offtheground.coffee

f @offthegrounduk   🐦 @offthegrounduk   📷 @offthegrounduk

65 KODA

17 Northway, Scarborough, North Yorkshire, YO11 1JH

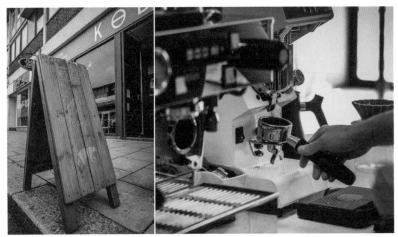

This multi-roaster coffee shop in the seaside town of Scarborough isn't a tick-it-off-the-list kind of place. Founder Reece Wilde created Koda to give customers the chance to try something different on every visit, while also being the kind of place they can drop in for a consistently great flat white.

'From day one we've wanted our customers to experience the best quality coffee possible and get them engaged with what they're drinking, rather than putting them off with too much information or jargon,' says Reece.

 CHECK OUT THE SEASONAL DRINKS MENU OF CREATIVE FLAVOUR COMBOS

The bill of hero roasteries that have taken a ride in the grinder since the cafe opened in 2019 is lengthy, and includes far-flung indies such as April Coffee (Denmark) and Expat (Bali). Alongside the globetrotting guests is a top-notch house coffee from Leeds' North Star.

Koda flies the flag for plant-based food and drink in Scarborough, so expect to encounter as many people visiting for lunch as for coffee. Check out the towering sandwiches stacked high with delish combos such as marinated tempeh, sauerkraut, grilled cheese and homemade Russian dressing.

ESTABLISHED
2019

KEY ROASTER
North Star
Coffee Roasters

BREWING METHOD
Espresso,
pourover

MACHINE
La Marzocco Linea

GRINDER
Mythos One,
Mahlkonig EK43 S

OPENING HOURS
Tue–Sat
9am–5pm

 Gluten FREE

 BEANS AVAILABLE INSTORE

 WIFI

 BRING YOUR OWN Cup

 DOG FRIENDLY

07921 511714
 @kodacoffeeshop @koda.coffee

66 YAY COFFEE!

Scarborough, North Yorkshire

The pandemic forced every small-business owner to think on their feet and possibly pivot the direction of their set-up. For the family team at Yay Coffee! their new route proved to be a winner.

Over the past six years Yay Coffee! has popped up at several bricks-and-mortar venues across Scarborough but when, in 2020, it was forced to close its HQ as a result of lockdown, the cafe went mobile instead. Luckily, founders Lottie and Rob already had a Bedford Rascal in their garage which, over lockdown, they converted into a coffee van to serve espresso at locations across the seaside town.

 HIRE THE YAY MOBILE COFFEE-SHOP FOR YOUR NEXT EVENT

The roaming cafe was such a hit the duo are now on a permanent mission to prove that quality coffee can be served on four wheels. A fully functioning La Marzocco Linea PB is installed in the back of the van, and used to craft silky espresso from Hasbean beans.

You'll usually find the van at Holbeck Clock Tower, but check social to keep up to date on its movements.

ESTABLISHED
2015

KEY ROASTER
Hasbean

BREWING METHOD
Espresso

MACHINE
La Marzocco
Linea PB

GRINDER
Nuova Simonelli
Mythos One,
Mahlkonig EK43

OPENING HOURS
Seasonal
(check website and social)

 BEANS AVAILABLE INSTORE

 CYCLE FRIENDLY

 OUTDOOR seating

 DISABLED ACCESS

 BRING YOUR OWN cup

 DOG FRIENDLY

www.yaycoffee.com   07946 517458

f @yaycoffeeuk   🐦 @yaycoffeeuk   ⊙ @yaycoffeeuk

67 TWO GINGERS COFFEE

5 Paragon Arcade, Hull, East Yorkshire, HU1 3PQ

Since 2017, Two Gingers has had one simple goal: to make great coffee.

Behind the stately shopfront, where huge windows are bordered by painted wood and bright tiles, the TG baristas work with the fruits of some of the best European roasteries to fulfil this mission. The chosen beans shift in line with regional harvesting seasons, and the team use precision brewing to highlight the characteristics of each coffee's terroir.

 SOURCE BEANS AND BREWING KIT FROM THE TWO GINGERS WEBSHOP

There's always a good selection of beans to choose from, prepared as espresso, batch or cold brew. Plump for the house roast from Scotland's Obadiah, or go off-piste via one of the guest roasts from Bonanza, La Cabra, Coffee Collective, Manhattan Coffee or Drop Coffee.

From Basque-style cheesecakes to rich truffle balls, a short but sweet curation of baked goods is made in-house to match customers' pick of the coffee list.

Those looking to brush up their brewing skills or finesse the craft of latte art should check out Two Gingers' online brew guides.

ESTABLISHED
2017

KEY ROASTER
Obadiah Coffee

BREWING METHOD
Espresso,
batch filter,
cold brew

MACHINE
Victoria Arduino
Black Eagle,
Slayer Espresso

GRINDER
Mythos One
x 2, Mythos 2,
Mahlkonig EK43

OPENING HOURS
Mon–Sun
10am–4pm

 BEANS AVAILABLE INSTORE

 CYCLE FRIENDLY

 DISABLED ACCESS

 BRING YOUR OWN Cup.

 COFFEE COURSES

 DOG FRIENDLY

www.twogingerscoffee.co.uk   07506 996989

f @twogingerscoffee   🐦 @twogingers_   📷 @twogingerscoffee

68 THE CURIOUS COFFEE COMPANY – HAXBY

Unit 8, Haxby Shopping Centre, Haxby, York, North Yorkshire, YO32 2LU

Four years after establishing The Curious Table in Easingwold, Eddie and Jenny Copley-Farnell opened their second North Yorkshire coffee house.

Community is at the heart of the operation, and the Copley-Farnells gave the takings from their first day of trading (£1,600) to charity St Leonard's Hospice, in memory of Eddie's step-grandfather Trevor.

 Insider's TIP TAKE A SECOND BITE OF THE EPIC BROWNIES AT HOME VIA THE ONLINE SHOP

The Haxby outpost is a big hit with locals for its expertly prepared coffee, roasted by York Emporium, which is served with a bite-size chunk of brownie from sister brand The Curious Brownie Company. Visitors can choose between the house espresso or one of the two roasts for AeroPress: Nicaraguan Santa Maria has notes of lemonade, milk chocolate and tangerine, while Sumatra Bener Meriah reveals nutmeg, raw honey and sweet tobacco flavours.

Pizza nights go down on an ad-hoc basis, so check social to find out when the next one is taking place. Eddie takes charge of the oven and turns out a series of showstoppers, including It's All White – a bechamel base topped with garlic oil, mozzarella, rocket, grana padano and parma ham. Pair your pick of the pizzas with a tipple from the new drinks menu of wines, craft beers and spirits.

ESTABLISHED
2017

KEY ROASTER
York Emporium

BREWING METHOD
Espresso,
AeroPress,
french press

MACHINE
Cimbali M39

GRINDER
Faema MD3000

OPENING HOURS
Mon-Fri
7.30am-4pm
Sat
8.30am-4pm
Sun
9.30am-3pm

 Gluten FREE

 BEANS AVAILABLE INSTORE

 WIFI

 CYCLE FRIENDLY

 OUTDOOR SEATING

 BRING YOUR OWN CUP

COFFEE COURSES

 DOG FRIENDLY

---

www.curiouscoffee.co **01904 765158**
f @thecuriouscoffeecompany 🐦 @curiouscoffeeed 📷 @curiouscoffeehaxby

69 THE CURIOUS COFFEE COMPANY – EASINGWOLD

Market Place, Easingwold, York, North Yorkshire, YO61 3AG

The Curious Coffee Co started out in January 2014 as The Curious Table before it was rebranded in 2020. However, while it sports a new name, the same irresistible components that made the cafe an Easingwold institution remain.

Curious is best known for its brownies (produced by sister brand The Curious Brownie Company) which can be ordered online for sofa scoffing. The too-good-to-turn-down collection includes corner-shop faves such as Oreo, Mars, Twix, Double Decker, Toffee Crisp, Rolo and Mint Aero. Visitors who swing by the cafe for a brew are also treated to a bite-size chunk on the side.

 Insider's TIP
CHECK SOCIAL FOR DEETS ON THE NEXT PIZZA NIGHT

Coffee keeping the cocoalicious treats company is supplied by York Emporium in Nether Poppleton. The cafe's bespoke house blend, which features beans from Vietnam, Ethiopia, Brazil and Guatemala, provides nutty flavours with a hint of dark chocolate. AeroPress offerings include Santa Maria, a Nicaraguan coffee with notes of lemonade, milk chocolate and tangerine.

If the complimentary baby brownie doesn't touch the sides, order something sizeable from the curiously good all-day brunch menu which includes french toast, eggs benny and posh beans on toast.

ESTABLISHED
2014

KEY ROASTER
York Emporium

BREWING METHOD
Espresso, AeroPress, french press

MACHINE
Cimbali

GRINDER
Cimbali Magnum

OPENING HOURS
Mon-Fri
7.30am-4pm
Sat
8.30am-4pm
Sun
9.30am-3pm

 Gluten FREE

 BEANS AVAILABLE INSTORE

 WIFI

 CYCLE FRIENDLY

 OUTDOOR seating

 BRING YOUR OWN Cup.

 DOG FRIENDLY

www.curiouscoffee.co   01347 823434
f @curiouscoffeeeasingwold   @curiouscoffeeeasingwold

70 BEAN & BUD

14 Commercial Street, Harrogate, North Yorkshire, HG1 1TY

© Leanne Peacock

This Harrogate coffee shop is a pioneer in the northern speciality scene and, for over a decade, has been somewhere to sample rare and interesting coffees that are often hard to find.

The team are clued up when it comes to speciality coffee and love to talk visitors through the current selection. There are usually at least six single-origin beans to choose from, with a strong showing of African and South American coffees. Sample them via a roster of different brew methods.

Insider's Tip THE NEWLY EXPANDED RETAIL SECTION INCLUDES BARISTA KIT AND BREWING ACCESSORIES

While the main focus is coffee, the tea offering is just as specialist. Over 20 loose-leaf varieties line the shelves and come with recommended brew times. There's also a line-up of single origin and organic hot chocolates.

Whatever you choose to sip, pair it with a tasty bite from the selection of locally sourced and homemade cakes, traybakes and pastries. There's a small menu of freshly prepped sandwiches, too, if you're after something more substantial.

ESTABLISHED
2010

KEY ROASTER
Multiple roasteries

BREWING METHOD
Espresso, V60, Chemex, AeroPress, Kalita Wave, batch brew

MACHINE
La Marzocco Strada EP

GRINDER
Mahlkonig K30, Mahlkonig Tanzania, Mythos

OPENING HOURS
Mon-Fri
8am-3pm
Sat
8am-4pm
Sun
10am-4pm

Gluten FREE

BEANS AVAILABLE INSTORE

WIFI

OUTDOOR seating

DISABLED ACCESS

BRING YOUR OWN Cup

COFFEE COURSES

DOG FRIENDLY

www.beanandbud.co.uk

f @beanandbud   🐦 @beanandbud   📷 @beanandbud

71 STARLING INDEPENDENT BAR CAFE KITCHEN

47 Oxford Street, Harrogate, North Yorkshire, HG1 1PW

Whatever the time of day or evening, this Harrogate coffee shop has a compilation of food, drink and vibes to suit the mood.

From opening until 2.30pm, brunch reigns supreme. Starling delights visitors with granola, coconut porridge, cooked brekkie blowouts and the house spesh: the three-egg slider (eggs benedict, eggs florentine and eggs royale, all on one plate).

 HEAD OUTSIDE TO PERCH UNDER THE STARLING MURAL

Kick-the-day-off coffee comes from Dark Woods in Huddersfield, whose award-winning medium roast Under Milk Wood is a joy pulled through the La Marzocco Linea and showered in steamed milk. This house staple is accompanied by an array of guest single-origin coffees from the likes of Origin, Caravan and Extract. Loose-leaf tea enthusiasts can get stuck into a selection from Manchester's Brew Tea Company.

When brunch winds down, a bar-like energy ramps up as 16 draft beers and ciders from independent northern breweries, plus the odd espresso, fuel evening frolics.

ESTABLISHED
2017

KEY ROASTER
Dark Woods Coffee

BREWING METHOD
Espresso,
V60, filter

MACHINE
La Marzocco Linea

GRINDER
Mahlkonig E65S,
Mahlkonig EK43

OPENING HOURS
Mon-Wed
9am-10pm
Thu-Sat
9am-11pm
Sun
10am-10pm

www.starlinghgte.co.uk   01423 531310

f @starlinghgte   🐦 @starlinghgte   📷 @starlinghgte

72 LAY OF THE LAND

Kings Mill Lane, Settle, North Yorkshire, BD24 9BS

Speciality beans and splendid blooms might be an unusual duo of delights but this bijou garden centre in Settle happily combines the two. After wandering the aisles lusting over the beautiful flora, visitors can pop into the cafe to sample Bradford-roasted Casa Espresso coffee served as espresso, AeroPress or pourover.

There's always something new to sip in this freshly refurbished contemporary space: beans get switched up every few weeks to reflect seasonal harvests, while a decent selection of loose-leaf teas promises quality cuppas.

 DIG INTO BREAKFAST, LUNCH AND AFTERNOON TREATS

It's not just plants and coffee that are well tended at this family-run set-up. Youngest son James 'Jimmie' Lay, who trained at Michelin-starred Northcote in Langho, sees to it that pretty much everything is homemade using kitchen-garden or locally supplied produce. Even the secret-recipe ketchup slathered on the bacon butties is rustled up in-house.

ESTABLISHED
2015

KEY ROASTER
Casa Espresso

BREWING METHOD
Espresso,
AeroPress,
pourover

MACHINE
Victoria Arduino
Eagle One

GRINDER
Victoria Arduino
Mythos One,
Sanremo SR70 EVO

OPENING HOURS
Mon-Sat
9am-4.30pm
Sun
10am-3pm

 Gluten FREE

 BEANS AVAILABLE INSTORE

 WIFI

 CYCLE FRIENDLY

 OUTDOOR seating

 DISABLED ACCESS

BRING YOUR OWN Cup

 DOG FRIENDLY

www.layoftheland.co.uk   01729 824247

f @layofthelandsettle   🐦 @lay_of_the_land   📷 @layoftheland_settle

73 BEAN LOVED

17 Otley Street, Skipton, North Yorkshire, BD23 1DY

Serving top-notch flat whites and long blacks since 2007, Bean Loved was the first speciality cafe in Skipton and continues its mission to champion delicious and responsibly sourced coffee.

Rather than offering a menagerie of brewing methods and beans, founder Wes Bond focuses on producing consistently spot-on coffee served in one simple style. A longstanding partnership with Dark Woods in Huddersfield has resulted in a bespoke house blend which Bean Loved's skilled baristas use to fashion a reliably top-notch range of espresso drinks.

INSIDER'S TIP — LOVE THE COFFEE? PICK UP A BAG OF THE HOUSE BEANS TO BREW AT HOME

Food is where the Bean Loved team funnel their creativity, and the menu of brunch and lunch dishes is one of the best for miles. Can't decide what to choose? Follow the crowd and order the house favourite: sweet-potato fritter stack with poached egg, smashed avo, grilled halloumi and sriracha; or check out the shakshuka baked eggs with fiery chorizo and a wedge of locally baked sourdough.

If the weather's good, head outside to the newly refurbed seating area and do brunch alfresco.

ESTABLISHED
2007

KEY ROASTER
Dark Woods Coffee

BREWING METHOD
Espresso

MACHINE
La Marzocco GB5

GRINDER
Mythos One x 2

OPENING HOURS
Mon-Thu
8am-3pm
Fri-Sat
8am-4pm
Sun
9am-3pm

  Gluten FREE
 BEANS AVAILABLE INSTORE
 WIFI
 OUTDOOR seating
 BRING YOUR OWN cup
  DOG FRIENDLY

www.beanloved.co.uk   01756 791534
f @beanlovedskipton   @beanloved   @beanloved

74 STEEP & FILTER

14 Otley Street, Skipton, North Yorkshire, BD23 1DZ

There seems to be no stopping the ambitious, ethically driven team at this plant-based cafe. Since opening in 2018 as an eco-friendly coffee and tea house, Steep & Filter has expanded twice: in 2019, it made room to include a refill store, then in 2020 it grew again to incorporate an organic greengrocers.

Alongside the retail arms of Steep & Filter, the cafe serves sustainably sourced plant-based food and drinks. Coffee comes courtesy of North Star in Leeds, whose Czar Street blend features on espresso while its seasonal single origins are served via filter. There's also a vast menu of loose-leaf teas, which includes everything from imperial pu-erh to organic white peony.

PICK UP A BAKERI BALTZERSEN SOURDOUGH LOAF TO TAKE HOME

Anyone who feels they're missing meat on the food menu will find the V-Bacon Sandwich to be an excellent alternative. The deceptively meatless creation consists of marinated tempeh rashers, mushrooms and red or brown sauce. Alternatively, try the Hash & Scrambles – a mound of savoury scrambled ackee and spuds.

ESTABLISHED
2018

KEY ROASTER
North Star
Coffee Roasters

BREWING METHOD
Espresso,
Moccamaster

MACHINE
La Marzocco
Linea PB

GRINDER
Fiorenzato
F64 EVO

OPENING HOURS
Tue-Sat
8am-3.30pm
Sun
9am-3.30pm

www.steepandfilter.co.uk   01756 795797

f @Steep&Filter   🐦 @steepandfilter   ⭕ @steepandfilter

75 THE CLUBHOUSE COFFEE & CYCLES

18 Newmarket Street, Skipton, North Yorkshire, BD23 2HR

Kane Pulford-Roberts fulfilled a long-held ambition of becoming his own boss when he opened The Clubhouse in July 2018. Originally from North Wales, Kane was working in Leeds prior to establishing his cafe and has clearly brought some city vibes to the market town of Skipton.

After just a year running the cafe, Kane decided to roast his own beans and set up The Clubhouse micro-roastery. Now his gaff is the only coffee house in Skipton serving own-roasted brews. Try the beans (sourced from all over the world, depending on what's in season) in the single-origin house roast.

 GONE NOON? ORDER THE NEXT-LEVEL ESPRESSO MARTINI

Coffee is prepped as espresso, batch and filter, and is best paired with something delicious from a selection of bakes. The house spesh is the Franzbrötchen, a spicy-sweet cinnamon-spiked German pastry.

The Clubhouse is a haven for bike lovers: professional cyclists such as Scott Thwaites and Olympic gold-medalist Tom Pidcock have visited, as have Olympic triathlete brothers Alistair and Jonny Brownlee.

ESTABLISHED
2018

KEY ROASTER
The Clubhouse
Coffee & Cycles

BREWING METHOD
Espresso, V60,
AeroPress,
batch brew

MACHINE
Victoria Arduino
White Eagle

GRINDER
Victoria Arduino
Mythos One

OPENING HOURS
Wed–Thu
8.30am–5pm
Fri–Sat
8.30am–9.30pm
Sun
10am–3pm

 Gluten FREE

 BEANS AVAILABLE INSTORE

 WIFI

 CYCLE FRIENDLY

 OUTDOOR seating

 COFFEE COURSES

 DOG FRIENDLY

www.theclubhousecc.co.uk   07808 831523
f *@theclubhousecc* 🅞 *@theclubhousecoffee*

76 TOAST HOUSE

22 Leeds Road, Ilkley, West Yorkshire, LS29 8DS

The team at Toast House are unashamedly devoted to all things toast, and celebrate it in all its golden glory. Slowly proved sourdough is the humble foundation on which Toast's innovative homemade masterpieces are crafted.

The crew take the art of coffee as seriously as the craft of baking, and have collaborated with respected Leeds roastery North Star to develop a bespoke espresso blend. Punters can also buy bags of single-origin beans from Malawian Coffee Co., a social enterprise supporting Malawi's remote coffee-growing communities.

 BAKING BREAD OR BREWING COFFEE? GRAB ALL THE GEAR TO-GO

For the Toast House team, doing good is just as important as creating good things. They're recipients of a Surfers Against Sewage plastic-free award, and are committed to reducing waste and increasing recycling at the cafe and through the lifestyle retail range.

The light and airy venue feels delightfully homely; chatter floats freely between bakers and diners. Freshly baked cakes capture visitors' attention, while shelves, sideboards and tables are filled with homewares and artisan foods for sale.

ESTABLISHED
2013

KEY ROASTER
North Star
Coffee Roasters

BREWING METHOD
Espresso

MACHINE
La Marzocco
Linea PB

GRINDER
Mahlkonig
K30 Air

OPENING HOURS
Mon–Fri
9am–3pm
Sat
9am–4pm
(seasonal opening hours)

 Gluten FREE

  BEANS AVAILABLE INSTORE

 OUTDOOR seating

 BRING YOUR OWN cup

www.toasthouse.co.uk   01943 601987

f @toasthouse   🐦 @toastilkley   📷 @toastilkley

77 TAMBOURINE COFFEE

38 Bingley Road, Saltaire, West Yorkshire, BD18 4RU

The Tambourine troupe continue to bang the speciality-coffee drum to lure people from all of parts of society to this Saltaire spot.

Tots are as welcome as keyboard-tappers, so whether you're carrying a nipper, a MacBook or the latest McEwan, you'll find a suitable spot in which to soak up the welcoming vibes.

PICK UP A HOME-COMPOSTABLE BAG OF HOUSE COFFEE TO-GO

The focus, as ever, remains on serving quality coffee. Leeds stalwart North Star provides the main roast, while a second hopper is filled with a feast of ever-changing flavours from the likes of Origin, Blossom, Square Mile, Cuppers Choice and Crankhouse. The guest roaster slot is switched up every fortnight so there's always something fresh to sample.

Brews can be paired with a smorgasbord of delicious edibles, including a surprisingly chunky range of savoury and sweet vegan options. Meet a mate for a brekkie of bhaji toasties – made in collaboration with the local curry house – paired with a sweet and bright single origin on filter to start the day with a bang.

ESTABLISHED
2017

KEY ROASTER
North Star
Coffee Roasters

BREWING METHOD
Espresso, filter

MACHINE
La Marzocco Linea

GRINDER
Mahlkonig K30,
Mahlkonig EK43 S

OPENING HOURS
Mon–Sat
8am–5pm
Sun
9am–4pm

 Gluten FREE

 BEANS AVAILABLE INSTORE

 WIFI

 CYCLE FRIENDLY

 OUTDOOR seating

 DISABLED ACCESS

 BRING YOUR OWN Cup

 DOG FRIENDLY

www.tambourinecoffee.co.uk **01274 945870**
🐦 @tambourinecoffe 📷 @tambourinecoffee

78 FIKA NORTH

94 Otley Road, Far Headingley, Leeds, West Yorkshire, LS6 4BA

Thanks to its set-up as a fabulous coffee shop by day and cocktail bar by night, Fika North has become a popular hub in the leafy suburb of Far Headingley.

As it was only established in 2019, the family-run outfit experienced a pandemic-hit couple of years not long after opening. However, hard work, the support of the local community (the team did takeaway during lockdowns) and perseverance has seen Fika North grow bigger and better than ever.

Insider's TIP — REVVING UP FOR A NIGHT OUT? THE ESPRESSO MARTINIS ARE OFF THE SCALE

Attention to detail shines through in everything here, from coffee to food to boozy beverages. The house roast comes care of Casa Espresso, while guest coffees pop up from the likes of UE, Girls Who Grind and Echelon.

On the menu, sourdough toast has been swapped for fresh bagels made by local artisan bakers. Each one is filled to order, with options including a stonking pastrami bagel (also available with vegan pastrami) and the house speciality Skagen (a Swedish dish of prawns, crème fraîche, dill, chives and dijon mustard).

ESTABLISHED
2019

KEY ROASTER
Casa Espresso

BREWING METHOD
Espresso, batch brew

MACHINE
La Marzocco Linea PB ABR

GRINDER
Fiorenzato F64 EVO x 2, Wilfa

OPENING HOURS
Mon-Tue
9am-5pm
Wed-Sat
9am-10pm
Sun
9am-6pm

 BEANS AVAILABLE INSTORE

 WIFI

 CYCLE FRIENDLY

 OUTDOOR SEATING

 BRING YOUR OWN CUP

 DOG FRIENDLY

www.fikanorth.co.uk   01138 243489
f @fikanorthcoffee   @fikanorth

79 BOWERY

54 Otley Road, Headingley, Leeds, West Yorkshire, LS6 2AL

Bowery founders Sandra and Ged have created a home-from-home vibe at their Otley Road cafe. Guests can find a cosy spot, sip coffee made from Allpress beans, browse the collection of books and enjoy Ged's carefully compiled playlists. Upstairs, there's an art gallery (curated by Sandra), a designer-maker shop and space for those looking to get some work done.

To accompany the drinks, a modest but mighty food menu features sandwiches and salad plates, plus savoury bakes and sweet treats. Despite competition from locally made ice cream it's actually the hearty salad plates that are the regular sellouts – choose from Cryer and Stott pork pie, organic falafel and hummus, or Bondage Bakery quiche, accompanied by Bowery seasonal salad compilations.

 BOWERY STOCKS FIVE SCRUMPTIOUS FLAVOURS OF NORTHERN BLOC ICE CREAM

In 2021, the team completed the design and build of a garden area so customers can sit and sip alfresco. There's plenty to keep little ones occupied too, including a sandpit and toys.

ESTABLISHED
2008

KEY ROASTER
Allpress Espresso

BREWING METHOD
Espresso, filter

MACHINE
La Marzocco
Linea Classic

GRINDER
Mazzer Major
Electronic

OPENING HOURS
Mon–Sun
9am–4pm

 Gluten FREE

 BEANS AVAILABLE INSTORE

 WIFI

 OUTDOOR seating

 BRING YOUR OWN Cup

 COFFEE COURSES

www.thebowery.org   01132 242284

f @boweryleeds   🐦 @theboweryarts   📷 @boweryleeds

8○ COFFEE ON THE CRESCENT

2 The Crescent, Hyde Park, Leeds, West Yorkshire, LS6 2NW

Inspired by speciality coffee venues he'd visited around the world, ex-professional cricketer and self-professed coffee snob Timothy Linley established this neighbourhood coffee shop near Hyde Park in 2019.

Coffee on the Crescent is Timothy's ode to the city's rich coffee-roasting culture: local roasteries Echelon, North Star and Maude feature on the sleek bar, alongside a line-up of limited-edition Coffee on the Crescent beans. The latest house release is Ethiopian single origin Birdcage, which was crafted to celebrate the new community garden recently created by Timothy and team on a piece of wasteland next to the cafe.

insider's TIP DON'T LEAVE WITHOUT TRYING 'THE BEST BROWNIES IN TOWN'

As well as establishing the communal garden, the COTC squad raised over £2,000 for a local foodbank during lockdown.

Pop by to sample the current single-origin fave, chased by a flaky almond croissant or pork-and-apple sausage roll. The chance to pick up other lovely provisions, such as locally baked sourdough, free-range eggs and organic butter, make taking a canvas shopper a no-brainer.

ESTABLISHED
2019

KEY ROASTER
Echelon Coffee Roasters

BREWING METHOD
Espresso, batch brew

MACHINE
La Marzocco Linea AV

GRINDER
Fiorenzato F64

OPENING HOURS
Mon-Sat
8.30am-4.30pm
Sun
9am-4.30pm

Gluten FREE

BEANS AVAILABLE
INSTORE

OUTDOOR seating

BRING YOUR OWN Cup

COFFEE COURSES

DOG FRIENDLY

---

www.coffeeonthecrescent.co.uk   01132 160380

f @coffeeonthecrescentleeds   🐦 @coffeepilgrimuk   📷 @coffeeonthecrescent

81 DOT THE LIONS

Leeds Arts University, Blenheim Walk, Leeds, West Yorkshire, LS2 9AQ

S tudents are often portrayed as greasy-spoon-loving penny pinchers, but the popularity of this speciality coffee shop at Leeds Arts University suggests that idea is somewhat outdated.

The takeout set-up is located in the foyer of the university, so members of the public queue with students and lecturers for quality espresso and wholesome food. The statement branding was created by a former student when the cafe was established in 2018.

FRESH PASTRIES FROM BAKERI BALTZERSEN IN HARROGATE ARE DELIVERED EVERY MORNING

As you'd expect from a sister venue to the excellent Laynes in central Leeds, the coffee is top-notch and roasted by the exceptional Dark Woods team in Huddersfield. Take a reusable cup and the pro baristas will pour your choice of espresso drink straight into it to save adding another paper cup to landfill.

The small food offering has a veggie/vegan leaning and includes colourful salads and artisan ciabattas. Swing by before breakfast to pick up a granola pot or chia pudding to go with a perfectly poured flat white.

ESTABLISHED
2018

KEY ROASTER
Dark Woods Coffee

BREWING METHOD
Espresso, batch brew

MACHINE
Synesso S200

GRINDER
Victoria Arduino Mythos One

OPENING HOURS
Mon-Fri
8.30am-4pm

Gluten FREE

CYCLE FRIENDLY

DISABLED ACCESS

www.dotthelions.co.uk   07828 823189
f @dotthelions   @dotthelions   @dotthelions

82 ARCHIVE

94 Kirkstall Road, Leeds, West Yorkshire, LS3 1HD

The actors and production teams who create TV programmes and indie films at Leeds' Prime Studios don't have to settle for awful catering-style coffee, thanks to this on-site cafe-meets-bar.

Housed in ITV's former archive, the speciality coffee spot is also open to the public, who swing by for morning brews, lunch and post-work drinks.

 HIRE THE ROOMY EVENTS SPACE FOR YOUR NEXT SPECIALITY-FUELLED KNEES-UP

The A-list house beans that stock the main grinder are sourced from Casa Espresso, although other red-carpet roasteries such as Hard Lines, Echelon and Square Mile make guest appearances throughout the year. Amateurs wanting to polish their brew skills at home will find beans from the roasteries available to purchase at the yellow-brick bar.

Between takes, stars join regular punters to chow down on appetising brunch and lunch dishes from the small but perfectly formed menu of edibles. Avocado and pickled red onions on sourdough, wild mushroom and smoked cheddar toasties, and spicy homemade beans on toast are so good most people return for a second take.

ESTABLISHED
2019

KEY ROASTER
Casa Espresso

BREWING METHOD
Espresso, cold brew, pourover, filter

MACHINE
Synesso MVP Hydra

GRINDER
Slingshot C68

OPENING HOURS
Mon-Tue
10am-3pm
Wed-Thu
10am-10pm
Fri-Sat
10am-late
Sun
10am-6pm

 Gluten FREE

 BEANS AVAILABLE INSTORE

 WIFI

 BRING YOUR OWN Cup

 CYCLE FRIENDLY

 OUTDOOR seating

 DISABLED ACCESS

 DOG FRIENDLY

www.archiveleeds.co.uk   07444 710139

f @archiveleeds   🐦 @archiveleeds   📷 @archiveleeds

83 STAGE ESPRESSO & BREW BAR

41 Great George Street, Leeds, West Yorkshire, LS1 3BB

At Stage, the spotlight is unashamedly and wholeheartedly on the star of the show: the coffee. Since 2017, the team at the brew bar in the heart of Leeds have showcased some of the world's best coffees sourced from the finest UK and European roasteries.

Tucked away on Great George Street, the coffee shop offers a brief interval from the daily grind. As calm descends and the coffee percolates, settle in and let the aroma revive your senses while the baristas work their magic.

IN A HURRY? GRAB A BALTZERSEN'S ALMOND CROISSANT AND BATCH BREW TO-GO

Choosing from the brew bar menu won't be easy – this is, after all, a coffee shop dedicated to introducing coffee fans to new and interesting beans. However, the baristas happily help stumped customers who can't decide what to imbibe from a selection that includes beans from Round Hill, Hasbean, Hundred House and Manhattan.

The food menu hones in on a handful of brunch favourites, freshly prepared using locally sourced produce. Sweetcorn fritters stacked with halloumi, aubergine kasundi and pesto are a firm favourite. Round off your visit with a knockout pastry, delivered daily from Baltzersen's in Harrogate.

ESTABLISHED
2017

KEY ROASTER
Multiple roasteries

BREWING METHOD
Espresso,
Kalita Wave,
Clever Dripper,
batch brew

MACHINE
La Marzocco GB5 S

GRINDER
Victoria Arduino
Mythos One,
Mahlkonig EK43

OPENING HOURS
Mon–Fri
8.30am–3pm

 BEANS AVAILABLE INSTORE

 WIFI

 BRING YOUR OWN Cup

 DOG FRIENDLY

www.stagecoffee.com
f @stagecoffee *@ @stagecoffeeleeds*

84 KAPOW COFFEE

15 Thornton's Arcade, Leeds, West Yorkshire, LS1 6LQ

Brew fans visiting Leeds should make a beeline for Kapow's flagship coffee shop, which is tucked away in the city's oldest covered shopping street. Thornton's Arcade is a slice of Victorian Leeds and a pleasing counterpoint to Kapow's 21st-century styling and its baristas' up-to-the-minute coffee knowledge.

Kapow's signature blend is own roasted and made from a balanced mix of Brazil Fazenda do Salto and India Chandragiri Natural beans. A pleasing all-rounder, it delivers the goods when served black on V60 just as well as it does when pulled through the Sanremo and served as espresso paired with milk. Expect to encounter a nutty, chocolatey base with notes of sweet dried fruit.

 CHECK OUT KAPOW'S SISTER COFFEE SHOP AT THE CALLS

The house fave is kept company by a large and ever-changing range of beans from guest roasters such as Hasbean, Round Hill, Colonna, UE, Dark Woods and (Leeds local) Chipp. Drink your choice of coffee in, or buy a bag of beans to-go; the baristas will even grind them to suit your home set-up.

ESTABLISHED
2013

KEY ROASTER
Kapow Coffee

BREWING METHOD
Espresso, V60, batch filter

MACHINE
Sanremo

GRINDER
Mahlkonig

OPENING HOURS
Mon-Sat
8am-6.30pm
Sun
10am-4pm

BEANS AVAILABLE INSTORE

 WIFI

 BRING YOUR OWN Cup.

 DISABLED ACCESS

---

www.kapowcoffee.co.uk

f @kapowthorntons   🐦 @kapowcoffee   📷 @kapowcoffee

85 LAYNES ESPRESSO

16 New Station Street, Leeds, West Yorkshire, LS1 5DL

For over a decade, Laynes has been the first stop on any coffee fan's tour of the caffeine-rich city of Leeds.

The pioneering coffee shop is located a 30-second dash from Leeds train station, so since 2011 (skirting over the bump that was 2020) there's been an almost constant stream of commuters dropping in for quality espresso. It's one of the most reliable stops for top-notch coffee in the city, and the regularly shifting roll call of guest beans features roasting royalty such as Dark Woods, Square Mile and Hard Lines.

 DON'T LEAVE WITHOUT TRYING THE VEGAN SOFT-SERVE ICE CREAM

While Laynes' enviable reputation was built on speciality coffee, in the past few years the team have also earned kudos for their brunch offering. The same quality and consistent approach that goes into every flat white has been adopted in the creation of dishes such as kale and spring onion bubble and squeak with fried eggs and roasted tomatoes, and fritters with spiced kasundi. Brunch gets pretty busy so book a table online in advance to avoid disappointment.

ESTABLISHED
2011

KEY ROASTER
Square Mile
Coffee Roasters

BREWING METHOD
Espresso, pourover,
batch brew

MACHINE
Synesso MVP

GRINDER
Mahlkonig E65S
GBW

OPENING HOURS
Mon–Fri
7.30am–3pm
Sat
8am–5pm
Sun
9am–4pm

 Gluten FREE

 BEANS AVAILABLE INSTORE

 WIFI

 BRING YOUR OWN Cup

 DOG FRIENDLY

www.laynesespresso.co.uk   07828 823189

f @laynesespresso   🐦 @laynesespresso   📷 @laynesespresso

86 OUT OF THE WOODS – GRANARY WHARF

Watermans Place, Granary Wharf, Leeds, West Yorkshire, LS1 4GL

Sister to the original Out of the Woods coffee shop on Water Lane, this venue shares the same cosy woodland-esque vibe and welcoming atmosphere. Located beside the canal, and not far from Leeds train station, it's a perfect pit-stop or journey's end for train hoppers, dog walkers and bike riders.

The two venues also share a fresh and wholesome menu which puts local produce front and centre. Check it out in hearty doorstep sandwiches (stuffed with the likes of Yorkshire roast ham, cheese, wholegrain mustard, tomato chutney and spinach) and decadent traybakes (the salted-caramel millionaire's shortbread is unreal) from Brown & Blond and White Rose Bakes.

 ASK FOR SOME OF OWNER ROSS' MUM'S CHUTNEY ON YOUR HAM SARNIE

Like the food, coffee is sourced locally. The house roast is crafted by Dark Woods: a multi-award-winning Huddersfield roastery that's dedicated to ethically sourcing fully traceable beans. Noteworthy guest coffees from Girls Who Grind, Obadiah and Coaltown offer batch filter alternatives.

ESTABLISHED
2010

KEY ROASTER
Dark Woods Coffee

BREWING METHOD
Espresso,
batch filter

MACHINE
La Marzocco
Linea PB

GRINDER
Mahlkonig K30

OPENING HOURS
Mon-Fri
7am-4pm
Sat
9am-4pm
Sun
9am-2pm

  Gluten FREE

 BEANS AVAILABLE INSTORE

  WIFI

 CYCLE FRIENDLY

 OUTDOOR SEATING

 DISABLED ACCESS

 BRING YOUR OWN Cup

 DOG FRIENDLY

www.outofthewoods.me.uk   01132 454144

f @outofthewoodsuk   🐦 @outofthewoodsuk   📷 @outofthewoodsuk

87 OUT OF THE WOODS – WATER LANE

113 Water Lane, Leeds, West Yorkshire, LS11 5WD

The original Out of the Woods venue (a sister cafe is at Granary Wharf) can be found a short drive out of the city centre amid the business hub of Water Lane.

It's here that worker bees from the surrounding companies flock to relax in a woodland-inspired setting, while refuelling with excellent brews and bites. Find them hunkered down inside on chilly days, sunning themselves on the outdoor seating in summer or grabbing lunch to-go.

 ### Insider's Tip KICKSTART YOUR DAY WITH THE SURFER-INSPIRED BRAZILIAN BREAKFAST

Locally made soups and salads sit alongside gooey grilled sandwiches on a menu that passionately celebrates Yorkshire produce. Even if you're only swinging by for a coffee, it's impossible to leave without pairing it with Brown & Blond brownie or a salted-caramel millionaire's shortbread from White Rose Bakes.

Fully traceable, ethically sourced speciality coffee from Dark Woods is always in the main hopper, while rotating guest beans from the likes of North Star and UE ensure even the most ardent regulars can continue to conquer new coffee horizons.

ESTABLISHED
2006

KEY ROASTER
Dark Woods Coffee

BREWING METHOD
Espresso, filter

MACHINE
La Marzocco
Linea PB

GRINDER
Mahlkonig E65S

OPENING HOURS
Mon-Fri
7am-4pm

 Gluten FREE

 BEANS AVAILABLE INSTORE

 WIFI

 OUTDOOR seating

 DISABLED ACCESS

 BRING YOUR OWN Cup

  DOG FRIENDLY

www.outofthewoods.me.uk   01132 448123
f @outofthewoodsuk   🐦 @outofthewoodsuk   📷 @outofthewoodsuk

88 SQUEEZE CAFE & DELI

19 Crown Street, Hebden Bridge, West Yorkshire, HX7 8EH

When Martha Howard opened her little cafe in 2007 she managed to squeeze a whole lot of deliciousness into its petite dimensions.

She and her team not only created a hub of heavenly coffee thanks to an extensive menu of expertly extracted espresso drinks, but also created a deli crammed with moreish delights, and a menu of Mexican-leaning dishes.

insider's Tip GO FULL MEXICO: ADD CAJUN CHICKEN OR BEAN CHILLI TO YOUR NACHOS

Pop in for an early morning caffeine pick-me-up crafted using Dark Woods beans, or plump for the likes of a Blueberry Mashup smoothie which wrings every bit of goodness out of the berries, banana, flaxseed and cranberry juice. There's also a stellar decaf roast from Casa Espresso.

Brunches include the perennially popular Big Squeeze wrap which is stuffed with grilled halloumi, Squeeze pesto, tomatoes, roasted peppers and leaves, or the ABC ciabatta (avo, bacon and chicken).

Press even more pleasure from your visit by purchasing something from a parade of pantry items, platters, hampers and foodie gifts, care of the deli.

ESTABLISHED
2007

KEY ROASTER
Dark Woods Coffee

BREWING METHOD
Espresso

MACHINE
Cimbali

GRINDER
Fiorenzato Pavelly, Ceado

OPENING HOURS
Mon-Sat
8.30am-4pm

Gluten FREE

BEANS AVAILABLE INSTORE

WIFI

DISABLED ACCESS

BRING YOUR OWN Cup.

---

www.squeezehebden.co.uk   01442 2471265

f @squeezehebden   @squeezehebden

89 COFFEEVOLUTION

8 Church Street, Huddersfield, West Yorkshire, HD1 1DD

This pioneering coffee shop has been a constant in the lives of Huddersfield locals for over two decades, and seen its regulars through everything from college and career changes to retirement.

Known as Evo to the locals, the cafe's friendly and longstanding baristas make it a truly welcoming space which even first-time visitors will find homely and relaxing. Step inside the statement-red building to be greeted by a beaming smile from behind an old-school counter that has the day's coffee menu chalked up on the wall behind.

 THE NEWLY PEDESTRIANISED STREET MEANS EXTENDED OUTSIDE SEATING

The stalwart house blend Derek is roasted across the city by sister company Bean Brothers Coffee. This Great Taste award-winning seasonal espresso combines three washed coffees from Africa and Central America and reveals notes of cocoa, almond and apricot. There's also a guest-roast slot filled by the likes of London's Dark Arts.

Grab a prime spot in the window and watch the world go by as you get stuck into one of the famed grilled-cheese sarnies made with local artisan bread, and a beer from the craft selection.

ESTABLISHED
2000

KEY ROASTER
Bean Brothers
Coffee Company

BREWING METHOD
Espresso, V60,
Chemex, AeroPress,
syphon, cold brew

MACHINE
La Marzocco FB80

GRINDER
Mahlkonig
K30 Twin,
Mahlkonig EK43

OPENING HOURS
Mon–Fri
7am–5pm
Sat
7.30am–5pm
Sun
9am–4pm

 Gluten FREE

 BEANS AVAILABLE INSTORE

 WIFI

 CYCLE FRIENDLY

 OUTDOOR seating

 DISABLED ACCESS

 BRING YOUR OWN Cup

 COFFEE COURSES

 DOG FRIENDLY

www.coffeevolution.co.uk   01484 432881

f @coffeevolution   🐦 @coffeevolution   📷 @coffeevolutionhuddersfield

90 ARCADE COFFEE & FOOD

9-10 Byram Arcade, Huddersfield, West Yorkshire, HD1 1ND

Skip breakfast before a visit to this Huddersfield venue as its homemade fodder is as big a draw as its speciality coffee.

The creative kitchen team rustle up an exciting all-day line-up of brunch, lunch and anything-in-between dishes, which range from comforting classics (toasted banana bread with peanut caramel, banana and cinnamon sugared almonds) to innovative must-tries (wild truffle mushrooms with truffle oil and cashew cream). There are also daily specials such as savoury waffles topped with seasonal ingredients (think fiery chorizo and spicy tomato salsa finished with a fried egg).

Insider's Tip: A HUGE SELECTION OF PLANT-BASED DISHES FEATURES ON THE ALL-DAY MENU

The homemade grub has garnered such a fanbase that chef Annabel and manager Blyth have established a regular supper club. The monthly events are themed and centre around locally sourced, in-season produce.

Arcade's coffee is worthy of just as much love. The team chose Arboretum from local roastery Dark Woods as the house espresso: its light roast reveals notes of chocolate and citrus, and shines when served with milk in a flat white. On batch brew, visitors can sample guest roasts from the likes of Girls Who Grind, Maude and Echelon.

ESTABLISHED
2017

KEY ROASTER
Dark Woods Coffee

BREWING METHOD
Espresso, batch filter

MACHINE
La Marzocco Linea Classic

GRINDER
Cimbali Magnum, Mahlkonig EK43

OPENING HOURS
Mon-Sat
8am-4pm
Sun
10am-4pm

Gluten FREE

BEANS AVAILABLE INSTORE

WIFI

OUTDOOR seating

DISABLED ACCESS

BRING YOUR OWN cup

DOG FRIENDLY

01484 511148
f @arcadecoffeefood   @ @arcadecoffeefood

91 WIRED COFFEE AND CAKE

17 Church Street, Honley, Holmfirth, West Yorkshire, HD9 6AH

Located on a quintessentially English cobbled street, Wired Coffee and Cake is a wonderful spot for whiling away the hours with a brew and a bake.

The team, led by founders Oliver and Katie, pair their house coffee from Dark Woods in Huddersfield with an ever-changing array of freshly baked goodies, from friands to flapjacks and traybakes to mini loaf-cakes. The indie cafe started out as an award-winning wedding cake business so you'd be bonkers to pass on its delicious creations.

 ASK WHICH GUEST ROASTERY IS CURRENTLY ROCKING THE SECOND GRINDER

For those firmly in the savoury camp, there's a selection of breakfast, lunch and brunch options, which have recently been made available as takeaway items too. Think egg and bacon butties and stacks of loaded toast and you're on the right track.

Check out the small but smart retail section, where you'll find bags of beans from a rotating range of speciality roasters alongside jars of preserves and indulgent peanut butters.

ESTABLISHED
2018

KEY ROASTER
Dark Woods Coffee

BREWING METHOD
Espresso, drip, V60, AeroPress

MACHINE
Iberital Expression Pro

GRINDER
Mahlkonig K30, Macap

OPENING HOURS
Fri–Sun
10am–3pm

 Gluten FREE

 BEANS AVAILABLE INSTORE

WIFI

 CYCLE FRIENDLY

 OUTDOOR seating

 BRING YOUR OWN Cup.

www.wiredcoffeeandcake.co.uk   07598 931448

f @wiredcoffeeandcake   🐦 @wiredcoffeeand1   ⊙ @wiredcoffeeandcake

92 BLOC

19a Huddersfield Road, Holmfirth, West Yorkshire, HD9 2JR

Few places reach out onto the pavement to welcome visitors in quite the same way as this Holmfirth favourite. The yellow awning and joyful window art (by Myro Doodle) beckon passersby through the outdoor seating into the bright cafe, where white walls with accents of wood and yellow hint at the food at its heart: toast.

Locally sourced artisan bread from Roger's Bakery in Marsden is stacked with an array of fresh ingredients that take toast from breakfast bonanza (brekkie-themed combos include chorizo, barbecue beans and egg) through to all-day extravaganzas such as avocado, halloumi and sweet-chilli salsa.

THE CARAMAC COOKIES ARE A DELICIOUS SHOT OF NOSTALGIA

Coffee is served as espresso (via an attention-grabbing custom yellow La Marzocco) and V60 pourover. Most people plump for the house roast from Dark Woods in Huddersfield, although a guest Brazilian and Costa Rican blend made especially for Bloc by local roastery BEAR is definitely worth a shot.

Home Sweet Holmfirth supplies the next-level collection of countertop cakes. In lockdown they were part of the lure that resulted in hour-long queues for top-notch takeaway coffee and indulgent baked goodies.

ESTABLISHED
2016

KEY ROASTER
Dark Woods Coffee

BREWING METHOD
Espresso, V60

MACHINE
La Marzocco Linea Classic

GRINDER
Mahlkonig K30

OPENING HOURS
Wed–Sun
9am–3pm

 Gluten FREE

 BEANS AVAILABLE INSTORE

 WIFI

 CYCLE FRIENDLY

 OUTDOOR SEATING

 DISABLED ACCESS

 BRING YOUR OWN cup

 DOG FRIENDLY

www.bloctoast.co.uk   01484 687228
f @blocholmfirth   🐦 @bloc_toast   📷 @bloc_toast

93 KRA:FT KOFFEE

12 Wood Street, Wakefield, West Yorkshire, WF1 2ED

KRA:FT's first customers only discovered it on visiting the tattoo artists and barbers with which it shared building space when it started out as a pop-up. However, word spread that the flat whites were as good as the fades, so the KRA:FT team took up permanent residence on Wood Street to make room for their growing following.

The new space has an industrial-glam vibe that's all copper, wood and leather – it perfectly fits KRA:FT's dual personality as both a coffee shop and cocktail bar.

 PAIR YOUR COFFEE WITH A KRONUT – THE FLAVOUR COMBOS CHANGE MONTHLY

By day, the gang serve a feast of bakes, craft beers and speciality coffee (courtesy of North Star, plus some of the UK's roasting greats who take turns on the guest grinder). Buy a HuskeeCup and enjoy a drink on the house while you do your bit for the planet. Brightly coloured matcha and beetroot lattes provide another draw.

By night, the lights are dimmed and the coffee cups swapped for coupe glasses. Coffee is still king, of course, and guests can savour speciality beans in the form of Espresso Martinis.

ESTABLISHED
2020

KEY ROASTER
North Star
Coffee Roasters

BREWING METHOD
Espresso,
filter, V60

MACHINE
La Marzocco
Modbar

GRINDER
Mythos 2,
Mahlkonig EK43

OPENING HOURS
Mon–Sat
8am–3pm
Sun
10am–3pm

 Gluten FREE
 BEANS AVAILABLE INSTORE
 WIFI
 CYCLE FRIENDLY
 OUTDOOR seating
 BRING YOUR OWN Cup
 COFFEE COURSES
 DOG FRIENDLY

www.kraftwakefield.co.uk   07921 180287
f @kraftkoffee @kraftkoffee

94 OLD GEORGE COFFEE HOUSE

14 Market Hill, Barnsley, South Yorkshire, S70 2QE

Founded in 2017, this is the original Old George Coffee House – its sister outposts are to be found at Town Hall and Wellington Mills in Huddersfield.

The team are clearly smashing their mission to bring banging brews and bakes to the area as the cafe collective has bagged a number of gongs – most recently Coffee Shop of the Year (South Yorkshire) in the 2021 Yorkshire Prestige Awards.

 IN A RUSH? PRE-ORDER YOUR TAKEAWAY COFFEE AND CAKE ONLINE

The Old George crew are all about raising the spirits of their customers, whether that's with great coffee, tasty food, friendly chat or a blend of all three. Their smile-inducing house espresso comes courtesy of Foundation (find more beans from the Cornish roastery on the retail shelves), while guest coffees from Square Mile are available for V60, AeroPress and batch brew.

For a sweet pairing, gooey brownies and towering cakes are just a couple of the storming temptations on offer from the in-house bakery. Heartier lunchtime options include the likes of chunky ciabatta rolls, warming soups and toasted wraps stuffed with local ingredients.

ESTABLISHED
2017

KEY ROASTER
Foundation
Coffee Roasters

BREWING METHOD
Espresso, V60,
AeroPress,
batch brew

MACHINE
Victoria Arduino
Eagle One

GRINDER
Mythos 2

OPENING HOURS
Mon–Sun
9am–4pm

 Gluten FREE

 BEANS AVAILABLE INSTORE

 WIFI

 OUTDOOR seating

 DISABLED ACCESS

 BRING YOUR OWN Cup

 COFFEE COURSES

 DOG FRIENDLY

www.old-george.co.uk   01226 695700

f @oldgeorgebarn   @oldgeorgebarnsley

95 THE WHALETOWN COFFEE COMPANY

227 Crookes, Sheffield, South Yorkshire, S10 1TE

When creating The Whaletown Coffee Company, Jordan O'Shea took inspiration from places that made him feel at home. So he's created a calm, warm and welcoming cafe which invites the Crookes community in to take a little time out.

Jordan also established Sheffield Coffee Festival and hosted the 2021 English AeroPress Championships, so visitors can feel assured they're in safe, experienced hands when it comes to procuring a quality brew.

FULL-ON DAY AHEAD?
ORDER THE FOUR-SHOT ORCA LATTE

Beans from Assembly Coffee in London are the house go-to and joined by a regularly updated selection of European and UK guest coffees – available as filter and espresso as well as bagged up for home brewing. Roasting greats Coffee Collective and Five Elephant make regular appearances.

A new development for Whaletown is the inclusion of micro-bakery Box Bakery+Kitchen to the coffee shop. Now diners can treat themselves to incredible sourdough bread and sourdough cookies (made using leftover starter) while sipping a perfectly crafted brew.

ESTABLISHED
2018

KEY ROASTER
Assembly Coffee

BREWING METHOD
Espresso, V60,
batch brew,
Kalita Wave

MACHINE
Victoria Arduino
Eagle One

GRINDER
Anfim Pratica x 2,
Ditting Swiss

OPENING HOURS
Mon-Sun
9.30am-4pm

www.whaletowncoffee.com   **07872 602232**

f @whaletowncoffeeco   ⃝ @whaletowncoffeeco

96 ALBIE'S COFFEE

22 Snig Hill, Sheffield, South Yorkshire, S3 8NB

Brother and sister duo Fraser and Robyn Hodges established this Sheffield coffee shop with the ambition of making good coffee accessible to all.

Since opening in 2018, Albie's has built a reputation for its friendly welcome, excellent coffee, fresh bakes and bulging made-to-order bagels. The coffee set-up is based around a stellar house espresso from Cuppers Choice (also in Sheffield) which is supplemented by a roster of guest beans (regulars include Artisan Roast, Crankhouse, Curve and Full Court Press) available as V60 and AeroPress.

Insider's Tip: WATCH ALBIE'S ONLINE BREW GUIDES OR RESERVE A SPOT AT ONE OF THE REGULAR BREW EVENTS

There are two espresso grinders – one for coffee blends suited to milk and another for single origins best imbibed black – and two filters on the go every day. If you like what you try, pick up the beans from the selection of bagged coffee to take home.

Make a morning visit to sample the king of the bagel menu: The Almighty. There's no better way to start a day than by sinking one's teeth into a glossy bagel crammed with grilled cheese, bacon, homemade potato rosti and a fried egg – served with a pot of baked beans on the side.

ESTABLISHED
2018

KEY ROASTER
Cuppers Choice
Coffee Roasters

BREWING METHOD
Espresso, V60,
AeroPress,
batch brew

MACHINE
La Marzocco
Linea Classic

GRINDER
Mahlkonig EK43,
Mazzer Kony,
Anfim Caimano

OPENING HOURS
Mon–Fri
8am–4pm
Sat
9am–4pm

Gluten FREE

BEANS AVAILABLE
INSTORE

WIFI

CYCLE FRIENDLY

OUTDOOR seating

DISABLED ACCESS

BRING YOUR OWN cup

DOG FRIENDLY

www.albiescoffee.co.uk

f @albiessheffield   @albiessheffield

97 MOW'S COFFEE

151 Arundel Street, Sheffield, South Yorkshire, S1 2NU

Launching in lockdown, Mow's Coffee came into existence when events and lifestyle space The Mowbray reached out to barista Sam Gilmer and proposed a partnership.

The street hatch, through which Sam served locals top-notch coffee while cafes remained closed, proved to be a life-saver for the new start-up and established the first Mow's Coffee regulars. It's still used daily to serve takeaway drinks to time-pressed passersby.

Inside, the hard lines of the red brick walls and antique marble counter are softened by vintage leather chairs, reclaimed timber and thriving houseplants. It's a refreshing alternative to the identikit coffee chains and a unique spot in which to cosy up with a good brew.

 GRAB A SLICE OF THE RICH PISTACHIO AND APRICOT FRANGIPANE

Sam worked with Dark Woods to develop two bespoke single-estate house coffees. The White Edition comes from Finca Esmeralda Diamond Mountain in Panama and tastes like bakewell tart thanks to its cherry, marzipan and dark chocolate notes, while the Black Edition is an Ethiopian coffee which reveals flavours of blueberry and lemon. The two house coffees sit alongside a roster of guest roasts and a small menu of delicious bites.

ESTABLISHED
2020

KEY ROASTER
Dark Woods Coffee

BREWING METHOD
Espresso,
pourover,
cold brew,
batch brew

MACHINE
La Marzocco
Linea PB

GRINDER
Anfim Pratica,
Mahlkonig EK43

OPENING HOURS
Mon-Fri
8am-5pm
Sat
9am-5pm
Sun
10am-4pm

 BEANS AVAILABLE INSTORE

 WIFI

 CYCLE FRIENDLY

 OUTDOOR SEATING

 BRING YOUR OWN CUP

 COFFEE COURSES

 DOG FRIENDLY

www.themowbray.co.uk/the-mowbray-cafe   07972 486851

@coffeeatmows

Roasteries

Yorkshire

98 ROOST COFFEE & ROASTERY

6 Talbot Yard, Yorkersgate, Malton, North Yorkshire, YO17 7FT

Roost was founded in 2015 by husband-and-wife team David and Ruth Elkington. Coffee is at the heart of the couple's work and family life – their passion for the bean has even percolated through to their children.

David and Ruth are very particular about sourcing coffee sustainably and ethically, and love to highlight the diverse coffees that arise through different varietals, soils, altitudes and processing methods.

ESTABLISHED
2015

ROASTER MAKE & SIZE
Joper BSR 15 KIT
15kg
Diedrich IR-12
12kg

CAFE ONSITE

OPEN BY APPOINTMENT

BEANS AVAILABLE
ONLINE ONSITE

'AN ON-SITE ESPRESSO BAR AND SHOP IS NESTLED AMONG ARTISAN FOOD AND DRINK PRODUCERS'

The North Yorkshire roastery always has at least three blends available at any one time, plus 12 single origins and a decaf. The latter is a hugely popular Guatemalan coffee that's crafted using the chemical-free Swiss Water Process. It delivers all the depth and character you'd expect from a Roost blend, but with a little less buzz.

An on-site espresso bar and shop is nestled among a handful of other artisan food and drink producers at Talbot Yard, making it an ideal one-stop destination for Yorkshire goodies. Call in to sink an espresso, chat to knowledgeable staff and pick up merch such as the new Roost cycle jerseys – en route you might spot David making local deliveries on the Roost e-bike.

---

www.roostcoffee.co.uk   01653 697635
f @roostcoffeeandroastery   🐦 @roost_coffee   📷 @roost_coffee

99 YORK EMPORIUM

Unit 4–5, Rose Centre, York Business Park, York, North Yorkshire, YO26 6RX

Those who seek the flavour-forward thrills of single-origin beans will find a huge collection to explore at this speciality emporium.

York's small team of coffee buffs roast a chunky selection of beans – there are around 40 available at any time – at their Yorkshire roastery. With two Q graders at the helm, the focus is on flavour and tickling out the intricacies of unique lots sourced from a plethora of bean-producing countries.

ESTABLISHED
2012

ROASTER MAKE & SIZE
Vintage Probat
25kg
Sivetz
20kg

'EDUCATION IS HUGELY IMPORTANT IN THE YORK EMPORIUM GRAND PLAN'

Coffees of note in the vast collection include Guatemala Red De Mujeres, an organic single origin produced by a women's cooperative in Huehuetenango, and The Clifford blend (named after York's famous tower) which reveals notes of citrus, milk choc and toffee. All the coffees are available to purchase from the York Emporium website, but the best way to really get stuck into the selection is via one of its three-monthly subscriptions.

Education is hugely important in the York Emporium grand plan and the team recently welcomed two new roasters, Matt and Lee, who completed their foundation course in 2021 and are now moving on to intermediate training.

---

www.yorkemporium.co.uk   01904 799399
f @yorkemporiumcoffee   🐦 @york_emporium   📷 @york_emporium

ATKINSONS

COFFEE ROASTERS

swift

J. ATKINSON & Co.

We're still standing
still independent
and still serving
Speciality Coffee

100 ECHELON COFFEE ROASTERS

Unit 20, Penraevon Industrial Estate, Penraevon Street, Leeds, West Yorkshire, LS7 2AW

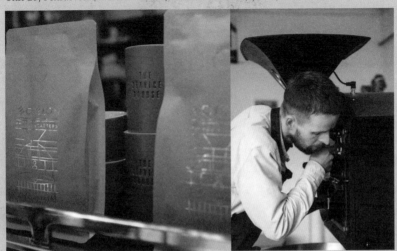

I n a Venn diagram of extra-curricular interests, coffee and cycling often overlap which, as the name suggests, is the case for Echelon owner Ben Craggs.

When he's not tackling two-wheeled pursuits, Ben roasts small batches of high-quality, sustainably sourced single-origin beans at his micro roastery in Leeds.

'Our philosophy is to showcase what makes each coffee unique,' says Ben. *'Our goal is to ensure all the hard work and dedication that farmers put into growing an exceptional product is fully expressed in every cup.'*

'OUR PHILOSOPHY IS TO SHOWCASE WHAT MAKES EACH COFFEE UNIQUE'

A truly seasonal approach to sourcing means beans from a huge selection of origins appear in Echelon's coffee subscriptions and online shop. In addition to seasonality, greens are chosen based on flavour, traceability and high ethical-standards.

In a further crossover with Ben's passion for cycling, the roastery has recently teamed up with Wilmslow cycle cafe The Service Course to create a bespoke seasonal single-origin espresso.

ESTABLISHED
2018

ROASTER MAKE & SIZE
Giesen W6A
6kg

OPEN
BY APPOINTMENT

COFFEE
COURSES

BEANS
AVAILABLE
ONLINE | OUTSETS

---

www.echeloncoffee.co.uk
f *@echeloncoffee* 🐦 *@echelonroasters* 📷 *@echeloncoffee*

HUDDERSFIELD

101 DARK WOODS COFFEE

Holme Mills, West Slaithwaite Road, Marsden, Huddersfield, West Yorkshire, HD7 6LS

The unwavering quality of Dark Woods' coffee is evidenced by numerous Great Taste awards – including two of its coveted Golden Forks (the food and drink equivalent of an Oscar) – and a shortlist inclusion in the BBC Food and Farming Awards (Best Drinks Producer 2021).

Since it was established in 2013, Dark Woods has blazed a trail of coffee beans across the North, pairing with cafes and restaurants to bring speciality coffee to the people. Its beans are also available online, direct from the roastery and via a network of artisan stockists, while the team's expertise can be tapped via their SCA-accredited courses.

'DARK WOODS HAS FORMALISED ITS COMMITMENT TO OPERATE AS A FORCE FOR GOOD'

As one of the first roasteries in the industry to be certified as a B Corp, Dark Woods has formalised its commitment to operate as a force for good. As such, it only sources fully traceable, ethically produced coffee of exceptional quality.

The Huddersfield roastery produces a diverse range of coffees, from crowd-pleasing blends to exclusive single-origin micro-lots for coffee connoisseurs.

ESTABLISHED
2013

ROASTER MAKE & SIZE
Probat G45
Vintage Probat
UG22 22kg
Probatone 5kg

COFFEE COURSES

COURSES

BEANS AVAILABLE

1O2 FRAZER'S COFFEE ROASTERS

46-47 Wilson Street, Neepsend, Sheffield, South Yorkshire, S3 8DD

Frazer Habershon doesn't only have nerves of steel: when he built his Sheffield roastery from scratch in 2014 (including constructing the actual roasters) he crafted his two 12kg machines using the city's famous metal.

This kind of attention to detail and dedication to graft and craft has resulted in a portfolio of top-quality coffees and four Great Taste awards.

'FRAZER CONSTRUCTED HIS ROASTING MACHINES USING THE CITY'S FAMOUS METAL'

Frazer bronzes his collection of popular coffee blends all year round, tinkering with the recipes to keep the flavours consistent. He also roasts a rotating collection of seasonal single-origin coffees, and is one of just a handful of UK roasters who make cold brew and nitro cold brew entirely in-house.

As someone who likes to build and create things, Frazer has a huge amount of respect for the farmers who produce the coffee beans he roasts. So, wherever possible, he tries to source directly to give the producers the maximum return for their toil.

ESTABLISHED
2014

ROASTER MAKE & SIZE
Handmade
12kg x 2

OPEN TO THE PUBLIC

COFFEE COURSES

BEANS AVAILABLE

---

www.frazerscoffeeroasters.co.uk   01142 015815

f @frazerscoffeeroasters   🐦 @frazerscoffee   📷 @frazerscoffeeroasters

KEEP THE

FEEL GOOD*

NEW BIG PACK

Arla

Lacto
FREE

SEMI SKIMMED
MILK DRINK

ALL NATURAL INGREDIENTS

PACKED WITH NUTRIENTS*

EASIER TO DIGEST*

FREE FROM LACTOSE

*Vit B12 contributes to the reduction of tiredness and fatigue. Calcium is needed for the maintenance of normal bones. Protein contributes to growth in muscle mass.

FLOWING

**SWITCH TO OUR NEW BIG PACK,
WITH MORE TO GULP, GUZZLE
AND SHARE AROUND**

103 FORGE COFFEE ROASTERS

Don Road, Sheffield, South Yorkshire, S9 2TF

The Forge team have been extremely busy since the last edition of the *North, Midlands & North Wales Independent Coffee Guide* was published.

The Sheffield roastery has continued to invest in new equipment and control systems to ensure its coffee is of the highest quality. This includes the purchase of a shiny new Giesen W1A roaster to further enhance and develop its range of blends and single origins.

'FORGE ENGINEERS CAN BE FOUND FIXING ESPRESSO MACHINES ACROSS THE REGION'

Although the team were kept busy with consumer orders during lockdown, their main focus is the commercial market. Forge is the La Marzocco distributor for Sheffield and surrounding areas, and its engineers can be found fixing espresso machines and coffee equipment at cafes and restaurants across the region.

The team also pop up regularly at events, where their fleet of modified vintage trucks – fitted with top-of-the-range espresso machines – are the source of silky flat whites and espressos for the lucky attendees.

ESTABLISHED
2015

ROASTER MAKE & SIZE
Giesen W30A
30kg
Giesen W15A
15kg
Giesen W1A
1kg

OPEN
BY APPOINTMENT

BEANS
AVAILABLE

---

www.forgecoffeeroasters.co.uk   **01142 441361**

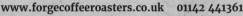
f @forgeroasters   🐦 @forgeroasters   📷 @forgeroasters

The Midlands

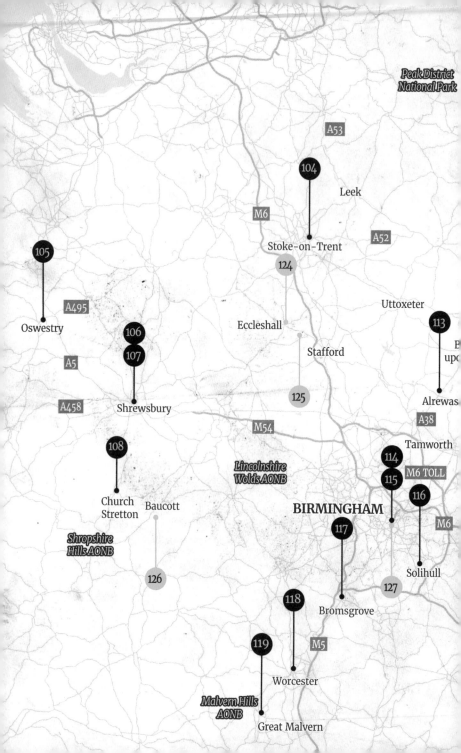

Peak District National Park

A53

104

Leek

A52

M6

Stoke-on-Trent

124

105

A495

Oswestry

Eccleshall

Uttoxeter

113

A5

106

107

Stafford

P
upo

125

Alrewas

A458

Shrewsbury

M54

A38

Tamworth

108

Lincolnshire
Wolds AONB

114

115

M6 TOLL

Church
Stretton

Baucott

BIRMINGHAM

116

M6

Shropshire
Hills AONB

126

117

Solihull

127

118

Bromsgrove

M5

119

Worcester

Malvern Hills
AONB

Great Malvern

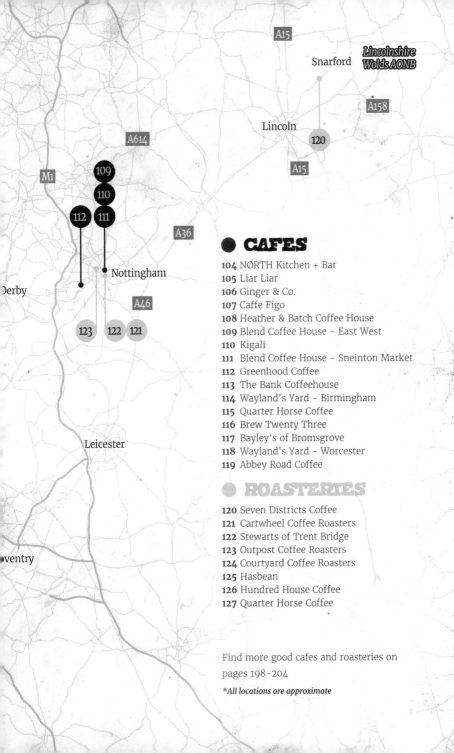

A15

Snarford   Lincolnshire
            Wolds AONB

A158

Lincoln

120

A15

A614

M1   109

            110

112   111

A36

Derby

A46

123   122   121

Nottingham

Leicester

Coventry

● CAFES

104 NØRTH Kitchen + Bar
105 Liar Liar
106 Ginger & Co.
107 Caffe Figo
108 Heather & Batch Coffee House
109 Blend Coffee House – East West
110 Kigali
111 Blend Coffee House – Sneinton Market
112 Greenhood Coffee
113 The Bank Coffeehouse
114 Wayland's Yard – Birmingham
115 Quarter Horse Coffee
116 Brew Twenty Three
117 Bayley's of Bromsgrove
118 Wayland's Yard – Worcester
119 Abbey Road Coffee

● ROASTERIES

120 Seven Districts Coffee
121 Cartwheel Coffee Roasters
122 Stewarts of Trent Bridge
123 Outpost Coffee Roasters
124 Courtyard Coffee Roasters
125 Hasbean
126 Hundred House Coffee
127 Quarter Horse Coffee

Find more good cafes and roasteries on
pages 198–204

All locations are approximate

104 NØRTH KITCHEN + BAR

31 Piccadilly, Hanley, Stoke-on-Trent, Staffordshire, ST1 1EN

The unmissable navy and white chevrons that decorate the outside of this attention-grabbing venue leave visitors in no doubt about where they need to head for good grub and brews.

Open from breakfast until late (midnight at the weekend), this is where the people of Hanley gather to indulge in Nordic-inspired food, drink and revelry.

Insider's Tip STAY IN THE SPIRIT – ORDER ANY OF NØRTH'S COCKTAILS TO-GO

Coffee comes fresh from a duo of London's roasting elite: the house roast courtesy of Climpson & Sons, guest beans from Dark Arts. Choose between espresso, drip, V60 and AeroPress, or iced alternatives when the sun shines on Staffordshire.

The food menu nourishes body and soul via dishes crammed with superfoods and nuggets of naughtiness in equal measure. Brioche toast topped with brown-sugar-baked pear, mascarpone, warm blackberries, maple-baked pecans and salted-caramel sauce is the kind of delicious fare we're talking about.

Those who worship the midnight sun can stick around to enjoy the relaxed, friendly vibe, awesome music and sensational coffee-cocktail specials.

ESTABLISHED
2015

KEY ROASTER
Climpson & Sons

BREWING METHOD
Espresso, V60, AeroPress, drip

MACHINE
La Marzocco Linea PB

GRINDER
Mythos One

OPENING HOURS
Thu
10am–10pm
Fri-Sat
10am–12am
Sun
11am–4pm

Gluten FREE

BEANS AVAILABLE
INSTORE

WIFI

OUTDOOR seating

BRING YOUR OWN Cup

DOG FRIENDLY

www.northcq.co.uk   01782 871299
f @northcq   @north_cq

105 LIAR LIAR

2 Albion Hill, Oswestry, Shropshire, SY11 1QA

The concept of a coffee house, gin bar and chicken-wing shop all operating under one roof seems implausible, but it makes sense when you take a seat at this Oswestry hangout.

Liar Liar shares its Grade II-listed home on the corner of Albion Hill and Bailey Street with House of Wingz (which deals in deep-fried buttermilk chicken wings and gravity-defying burgers) and speakeasy-inspired The Imitator Bar.

 THE HIDDEN CRAFT MARKET TAKES PLACE AT THE CAFE ON THE FIRST SUNDAY OF EVERY MONTH

The recent collaboration of businesses has resulted in an increase in the seating area from holding just 30 to room for 80 – welcome news for anyone who tried to squeeze into the original coffee shop.

Founder Thomas Jones introduced speciality coffee to the market town when he established Liar Liar. He continues to break new ground and recently added an extra grinder so he can provide two single origins plus an espresso blend. Hundred House is the key roaster but beans from other UK and European greats also feature.

ESTABLISHED
2016

KEY ROASTER
Hundred House Coffee

BREWING METHOD
Espresso, V60, batch brew

MACHINE
La Marzocco Linea PB

GRINDER
Mythos One x 2, Niche Zero, Mahlkonig Tanzania

OPENING HOURS
Mon-Sat 9am-4pm
Sun 9am-2pm

 Gluten FREE

 BEANS AVAILABLE INSTORE

 WIFI

 CYCLE FRIENDLY

 OUTDOOR seating

BRING YOUR OWN Cup

 COFFEE COURSES

 DOG FRIENDLY

www.liarliarcoffee.co.uk   **07845 666620**

f *@liarliaroswestry*   🐦 *@cafe_liarliar*   📷 *@liarliaroswestry*

106 GINGER & CO.

30-31 Princess Street, Shrewsbury, Shropshire, SY1 1LW

When Sam and Kate imagined the kind of coffee shop they'd like to open, they wanted to recreate the warm and friendly welcome Sam had as a child when he walked into his nans' houses. In 2015 they did just that – not in a farmhouse or a 1950s terrace, but an upcycled coffee shop in the heart of Shrewsbury.

Six years on, Ginger & Co. is a much-loved hub within the town. With an aim of making speciality coffee inclusive and accessible to all, Sam and Kate have created a space where everyone can feel at ease and enjoy great coffee, delicious food and homemade bakes.

insider's TIP THE BANANA AND CARAMEL CAKE HAS BEEN DESCRIBED AS 'EARTH SHATTERING'

The beans are roasted in Worcester by Mark and Tre at Method, who create a cracking house Market Blend for espresso, plus a line-up of single origins for batch brew. It's prepared by a rabble of friendly baristas who love to chat coffee with the customers as they pull the shots.

No nan would let anyone leave their house hungry, so of course there's a fab brunch menu and selection of cakes on offer. The new health-hit brunch bowls have been a huge success and include the likes of smoky bacon with smashed avo, heritage tomatoes, halloumi, spinach, pea shoots and homemade tahini dressing.

ESTABLISHED
2015

KEY ROASTER
Method Coffee
Roasters

BREWING METHOD
Espresso,
batch filter

MACHINE
La Marzocco
Linea AV

GRINDER
Mahlkonig K30,
Mahlkonig EK43

OPENING HOURS
Mon-Thu
8.30am-3pm
Sat
8.30am-4pm
Sun
10am-3pm

 Gluten FREE

 BEANS AVAILABLE INSTORE

 WIFI

 CYCLE FRIENDLY

BRING YOUR OWN Cup

 DOG FRIENDLY

---

www.gingerandcocoffee.com   07830 704090

f @gingerandcocoffee   🐦 @ginger_and_co_   📷 @ginger_and_co_coffee

107 CAFFE FIGO

16 Wyle Cop, Shrewsbury, Shropshire, SY1 1XB

The team at this Shrewsbury newbie weren't going to let the pandemic get in the way of their plans to open a new cafe in the heart of the town and, after a few setbacks, launched Caffe Figo on the proudly independent Wyle Cop in April 2021.

It's been an instant hit with coffee-loving locals. Bristol's Extract Coffee Roasters supplies a cracking espresso blend which provides a flavour-forward base for milk drinks thanks to its notes of caramel, cocoa, black cherry and liquorice. On decaf, its Sugarcane Espresso delivers flavour bombs of blackcurrant, brown sugar and cocoa.

 CHECK OUT THE LATEST GUEST ROAST FROM HUNDRED HOUSE IN SHROPSHIRE

Cakesmiths and Exploding Bakery stump up the baked goods that provide perfect coffee and cake pairings. The line-up of artisan brownies, traybakes and flapjacks changes seasonally and always includes a decent selection for plant-based visitors.

Those looking for more substantial eats will find sustenance in a small menu of freshly made paninis, salads and sandwiches.

ESTABLISHED
2021

KEY ROASTER
Extract Coffee
Roasters

BREWING METHOD
Espresso

MACHINE
La Marzocco

GRINDER
Mythos One

OPENING HOURS
Mon–Sun
8am–5pm

 Gluten FREE

 BEANS AVAILABLE INSTORE

 WIFI

 BRING YOUR OWN Cup

 DOG FRIENDLY

www.caffefigo.com
 @caffefigo @caffefigo

INDEPENDENT COFFEE BOX

INDYCOFFEEBOX.CO.UK

A curated selection of speciality beans from the UK's hero roasteries, delivered to your door each month – from £19.99.

108 HEATHER & BATCH COFFEE HOUSE

3 Sandford Avenue, Church Stretton, Shropshire, SY6 6BW

In the small market town of Church Stretton, located in the Shropshire Hills Area of Outstanding Natural Beauty, you'll find this red brick bolthole where mountain bikers and ramblers gather for quality refreshment.

Ahead of a trek up and down the tumbling hills, those in the know make tracks to Heather & Batch for freshly prepped food and flavour-forward brews. It's hard to beat a glossy shot of espresso crafted from beans bronzed at local roastery Hundred House, but those up for going off-piste can also sample a guest roast via the new second grinder.

 ON TWO WHEELS? PULL OVER: BIKE LOCKS CAN BE BORROWED FROM THE BAR

The all-day food menu is fresh, nutritious and stuffed with gratifying dishes to set visitors up for a day of adventures. Can't choose? Let us recommend one of the loaded breakfast baps (the avo, halloumi, bacon and chilli jam number is a good shout) chased by a chubby slice of blueberry-studded vegan bundt cake.

ESTABLISHED
2018

KEY ROASTER
Hundred House Coffee

BREWING METHOD
Espresso

MACHINE
La Marzocco Linea Classic

GRINDER
La Spaziale, Mahlkonig

OPENING HOURS
Mon–Sat
9am–4pm

 Gluten FREE

 BEANS AVAILABLE INSTORE

 WIFI

 CYCLE FRIENDLY

 BRING YOUR OWN Cup.

www.heatherandbatch.co.uk   01694 724644
f @heatherandbatch @ @heatherandbatch

109 BLEND COFFEE HOUSE – EAST WEST

East West, Toll House Hill, Nottingham, NG1 5FS

The latest addition to the Blend Coffee House family is at East West, a newly refurbished office block with a roomy cafe on the ground floor.

It's a grown-up version of Blend's original Sneinton Market outpost and caters for the office workers as well as nearby residents and passing coffee fiends.

ASK WHICH GUEST ROAST IS CURRENTLY ROCKING THE BATCH BREW SLOT

The bright and airy space certainly trumps the average working-lunch location. Blend's independent spirit softens the corporate setting, yet there are still plenty of plug sockets and potential workstations for those who want to whip out their laptop and catch up on emails.

The house coffee is expertly roasted by the team at Stewarts of Trent Bridge, who bronze beans at their roastery in Sneinton Market. Try the bespoke espresso blend as a flat white and choose between dairy milk or oat, hazelnut, tiger nut and split-pea alternatives.

Sandwiches, frittatas, filled croissants, salads and freshly baked cakes are served with speed to deliver the energy boost required by busy worker bees.

ESTABLISHED
2021

KEY ROASTER
Stewarts of
Trent Bridge

BREWING METHOD
Espresso,
batch brew

MACHINE
Conti MC Ultima

GRINDER
Compak E8

OPENING HOURS
Mon-Fri
8am-5pm

 Gluten FREE

 BEANS AVAILABLE INSTORE

 WIFI

 DISABLED ACCESS

 BRING YOUR OWN cup

www.blendnottingham.co.uk   01158 389350
f @blendateastwest   @blendateastwest

110 KIGALI

2 Stoney Street, Nottingham, NG1 1LG

Even the fussiest coffee fans will find something to light up their palates at this multi-roaster coffee house in Nottingham.

The Kigali crew love exploring different origins, processes and varietals, so there's always a huge variety of coffee choice available at the brew bar. The strictly single-origin offering includes two options on espresso, two on batch brew and two on manual brew, which are supplied by house roaster Outpost as well as a selection of guests.

 SAMPLE THE ESPRESSO SOFT-SERVE IN A NEXT-LEVEL ICE CREAM COOKIE SANDWICH

If the expansive coffee menu makes your head spin, the clued-up baristas are more than happy to talk through the prep options and tasting notes. They recently got their hands on an ice cream machine and have had a lot of fun perfecting their recipe for espresso soft-serve; grab one to-go for an entirely different speciality hit.

Visit early to have first pick of the golden pastries from fellow Nottingham indie Tough Mary's Bakehouse. An almond-showered Copenhagen Knot makes the perfect pairing to a flawless flat white.

ESTABLISHED
2020

KEY ROASTER
Outpost Coffee Roasters

BREWING METHOD
Espresso, V60, Clever Dripper, Moccamaster

MACHINE
La Marzocco Strada

GRINDER
Mazzer Robur, Mazzer Kony, Mahlkonig EK43

OPENING HOURS
Mon–Fri
8am–5pm
Sat
8am–6pm
Sun
10am–4pm

 BEANS AVAILABLE INSTORE

 WIFI

 OUTDOOR SEATING

 BRING YOUR OWN CUP

 COFFEE COURSES

 DOG FRIENDLY

07758 153315
@ @kigali_notts

111 BLEND COFFEE HOUSE – SNEINTON MARKET

Unit 30, Avenue C, Sneinton Market, Nottingham, NG1 1DW

This bright, spacious and family-friendly coffee shop sits in the heart of Nottingham's creative quarter.

Visit for impeccably fresh coffee which travels mere steps from the Stewarts of Trent Bridge roastery next door. The beans are skilfully transfigured, via Blend's Conti MC Ultima machine, into killer espresso drinks, although the talented barista team also craft batch brew and V60 filters. Nitro cold brew is available also on tap.

insider's TIP PEEK NEXT DOOR TO SEE WHERE THE HOUSE COFFEE IS ROASTED

Blend is known for its epic, comically named grilled cheese sandwiches, the foundations of which are locally baked sourdough and a bespoke cheese blend. Its take on welsh rarebit (Who Framed Roger Rarebit?) uses local Neon Raptor beer, wholegrain mustard and confit leeks to bolster the classic cheese sauce.

If that sounds a bit full-on, the selection of creative salads is just as enticing. Blend's current big-hitter features strawberries, toasted almonds, fresh basil and pickled fennel, with the option of goat's cheese or smoked chicken.

ESTABLISHED
2017

KEY ROASTER
Stewarts of Trent Bridge

BREWING METHOD
Espresso, V60, batch brew, nitro

MACHINE
Conti MC Ultima

GRINDER
Compak F8

OPENING HOURS
Mon–Fri
8am–5pm
Sat–Sun
9am–5pm

Gluten FREE

BEANS AVAILABLE INSTORE

WIFI

CYCLE FRIENDLY

OUTDOOR seating

DISABLED ACCESS

BRING YOUR OWN Cup

COFFEE COURSES

DOG FRIENDLY

www.blendnottingham.co.uk   01158 389350
f @blendnottingham   @blendnottingham

112 GREENHOOD COFFEE

38 High Road, Beeston, Nottingham, NG9 2JP

Since 2015, Greenhood Coffee has been slinging top-tier espresso for the people of Beeston. It was the first speciality coffee house in the area and still reigns supreme from its High Road home.

Set over two floors, the Japandi-inspired (Japanese meets Scandi) space is light and airy, creating a chilled environment in which to enjoy the Neighbourhood Blend: a fantastic all-rounder from specialist roasters Colonna in Bristol. There are also guest coffees from Oxford's New Ground, which rotate with Colonna on decaf, pourover and batch-brew duties.

 NO TRIP IS COMPLETE WITHOUT A VEGAN BUN – CHOOSE BETWEEN CINNAMON, CACAO AND MORE

Lockdown forced the team to get even more creative, resulting in what they've dubbed Greenhood ATW (at the window). An upgrade on the traditional drive-through, the take-out window is a one-stop shop for freshly prepped bagels, chunky cookies, pressed juices and, of course, top-notch coffee. Invest in one of the new Loyalty Cups to get £1 off every future hot drink purchased to-go.

ESTABLISHED
2015

KEY ROASTER
Colonna Coffee

BREWING METHOD
Espresso, April Brewer, batch brew

MACHINE
Kees van der Westen Spirit

GRINDER
Mythos One x 2, Mahlkonig EK45

OPENING HOURS
Mon-Fri
8am-6pm
Sat
9am-5pm

 BEANS AVAILABLE INSTORE
 WIFI
 CYCLE FRIENDLY
 DISABLED ACCESS
 BRING YOUR OWN CUP
  DOG FRIENDLY

 f @greenhoodcoffee   🐦 @greenhoodcoffee   @greenhoodcoffee

113 THE BANK COFFEEHOUSE

57 Main Street, Alrewas, Burton upon Trent, Staffordshire, DE13 7AE

When Jane Reilly opened a coffee house in this former bank building she created a second home for the Alrewas community, who check in daily to drink great coffee, catch up and kick back.

It's also popular with visitors who make a beeline for the village to explore the pretty canalside trails on foot and bike. As a result, the cafe's alfresco seats are sometimes packed with lycra-clad cyclists chugging espressos and tucking into plates of comforting homemade fodder.

 Insider's Tip: STICK AROUND ON FRIDAY EVENINGS FOR ACOUSTIC MUSIC SESSIONS

The beans fuelling the chatter and outdoor pursuits are supplied by Dark Woods in Huddersfield. Those used in the espresso drinks reveal notes of caramel, stewed fruits and praline thanks to the Under Milk Wood blend, while the decaf Lamplight delivers flavours of rich fruitcake and golden syrup. There's also always a guest option available which can be prepared as french press.

Skip brekkie before you visit so you've got what it takes to go full English. The Bank's version is stocked with local favourites from Coates Traditional Butchers (just across the road) and eggs from Jane's own brood of hens.

ESTABLISHED
2018

KEY ROASTER
Dark Woods Coffee

BREWING METHOD
Espresso,
french press

MACHINE
La Marzocco

GRINDER
Anfim Pratica,
Casadio, Wilfa

OPENING HOURS
Tue-Fri
9am-3pm
Sat
9.30am-3pm
Sun
10am-3pm

 Gluten FREE

 BEANS AVAILABLE
INSTORE

 WIFI

 CYCLE FRIENDLY

 OUTDOOR SEATING

 DISABLED ACCESS

 BRING YOUR OWN CUP

 DOG FRIENDLY

www.thebankcoffeehouse.co.uk   07722 891696
f @thebankalrewas   @ @thebankcoffeehouse

114 WAYLAND'S YARD – BIRMINGHAM

42 Bull Street, Birmingham, West Midlands, B4 6AF

Opposite Bull Street tram stop and just a few minutes from Snow Hill Station, you'll find Wayland's Yard. The spacious coffee shop sits amid the hustle and bustle of Colmore Row's busy business district, making it an ideal spot for informal meetings and solo laptop sessions as well as post-shopping debriefs and long lazy brunches with friends.

Much like at its sister sites in Worcester and Bristol, all-day brunching is the big draw. Egg-dipped crumpets topped with crisp salty bacon and cornflake fried-chicken, stacks of buttermilk pancakes, and skillet-pan hash are just a few of the house favourites which have become legendary among Wayland's loyal following.

 TRY THE SUGAR-DUSTED CINNAMON BUNS WHICH ARE BAKED IN-HOUSE EACH DAY

On the coffee front, beans are supplied by the house roastery (under the moniker Odd Kin Coffee Roasters) in Bristol, plus an ever-changing line-up of guests from the team's favourite roasteries. Explore the latest offering via AeroPress or V60, or simply pair a cracking flat white with one of the brunch dishes for a small slice of heaven.

ESTABLISHED
2018

KEY ROASTER
Odd Kin
Coffee Roasters

BREWING METHOD
Espresso, V60,
AeroPress

MACHINE
Victoria Arduino
Eagle One

GRINDER
Mahlkonig E80,
Mahlkonig EK43,
Mahlkonig E65S
GbW

OPENING HOURS
Mon–Sat
8am–4pm
Sun
9am–4pm

Gluten FREE

BEANS AVAILABLE INSTORE

WIFI

CYCLE FRIENDLY

OUTDOOR seating

DISABLED ACCESS

BRING YOUR OWN Cup

DOG FRIENDLY

www.waylandsyard.com

 @waylandsyardbirmingham    @waylandsyard   @waylandsyard

Take the *North, Midlands & North Wales Independent Coffee Guide* with you via the new app.

Find out more at:
indycoffee.guide/app

115 QUARTER HORSE COFFEE

88–90 Bristol Street, Birmingham, West Midlands, B5 7AH

Quarter Horse became Birmingham's first combined cafe and roastery when it opened the doors to its sleek, spacious eatery on Bristol Street.

Perfect for laptop surfing, brunching with friends and indulging your inner coffee nerd, it's a friendly space which balances industry excellence with modern design and a relaxed atmosphere.

FRESH CINNAMON BUNS COME WITH BOTH TRADITIONAL AND FLAVOURED GLAZES

Beans served in the cafe travel mere steps from the in-house roastery, and visitors can watch the roasting action as they sip their pick from the coffee menu. Choose between good-all-rounder espresso and rare single-origin roasts – there are also retail bags of beans for home-brewing experimentation.

The menu excels in cakes and light bites, while a small but tantalising brunch offering features freshly made and internationally inspired interpretations of morning and midday feasting. Dishes are updated regularly to include seasonal, local ingredients; however, returning visitors will be pleased to discover the breakfast baps and homemade cinnamon buns are Quarter Horse staples.

ESTABLISHED
2012

KEY ROASTER
Quarter Horse Coffee

BREWING METHOD
Espresso, Kalita Wave

MACHINE
La Marzocco KB90

GRINDER
Mahlkonig EK43, Victoria Arduino Mythos 2, Mahlkonig E65S GbW

OPENING HOURS
Mon–Fri
8am–6pm
Sat–Sun
9am–3pm

 Gluten FREE

 BEANS AVAILABLE INSTORE

 WIFI

 CYCLE FRIENDLY

 OUTDOOR seating

 DISABLED ACCESS

 BRING YOUR OWN Cup.

 COFFEE COURSES

 DOG FRIENDLY

www.quarterhorsecoffee.com   01214 489660

f @quarterhorsecoffee   🐦 @qtrhorsecoffee   📷 @quarterhorsecoffee

116 BREW TWENTY THREE

Cranmore Place, Cranmore Drive, Shirley, West Midlands, B90 4RZ

There's a lively, upbeat atmosphere at this Solihull hangout thanks to the super-friendly baristas serving knockout flat whites and fabulously fresh juices and smoothies – and the vibe is infectious. Whatever you order from the slick white-tiled bar is guaranteed to add a shot of positivity to your day.

Origin Coffee Roasters provide a washed house blend which is fashioned into Instagrammable flat whites to match the curated backdrop. A variety of seasonal guest beans from the Cornish roastery also feature.

 THE NEWLY REFURBISHED OUTSIDE SEATING IS SPOT ON FOR SUNNY DAYS

The ever-expanding list of made-to-order juices and smoothies is not to be missed. Take your time to peruse the creative line-up of fruity infusions and select the perfect chaser to your expertly pulled espresso.

Accompanying the drinks is a tempting selection of open sandwiches (served on attention-grabbing charcoal sourdough) and locally baked brownies and blondies. Post 12pm? Order a glass of organic natural wine with your lunch.

ESTABLISHED
2019

KEY ROASTER
Origin
Coffee Roasters

BREWING METHOD
Espresso

MACHINE
La Marzocco
Linea PB

GRINDER
Mahlkonig
K30 Twin

OPENING HOURS
Mon-Fri
7.30am-3pm
Sat
9am-3pm

  Gluten FREE
 BEANS AVAILABLE INSTORE
 WIFI
 CYCLE FRIENDLY
 OUTDOOR Seating
 DISABLED ACCESS
 BRING YOUR OWN Cup
  DOG FRIENDLY

07860 662979
f @brewtwentythree   @brewtwentythree

117 BAYLEY'S OF BROMSGROVE

6 Worcester Road, Bromsgrove, Worcestershire, B61 7AE

Since the last edition of the *North, Midlands & North Wales Guide*, this day-to-night destination has doubled in size, so now there's loads more space to sip great coffee and craft beer. The expansion has also resulted in a new kitchen which welcomes an ever-changing line-up of streetfood vendors on weekends.

By day, top-notch coffee from the likes of Birmingham's Quarter Horse and Bristol's Odd Kin is the focus of a team passionate about preparing every flat white, V60 or AeroPress like it's the first pour of the day. They're big on supporting local indies too, so milk for the cappuccinos and cakes that accompany the brews are all sourced from nearby artisan businesses.

 ON-TAP NITRO COLD BREW IS LINED UP FOR SUMMER 2022

As afternoon slips into early evening, the attention turns to craft beer and spirits. Browse the hefty selection of cans in the beer fridge, asking for a recommendation from the team if you don't want to be swayed purely by the eye-catching can art. More cocktails than craft beer? Order the Nitro Espresso Martini.

ESTABLISHED
2017

KEY ROASTER
Quarter
Horse Coffee

BREWING METHOD
Espresso, V60,
AeroPress

MACHINE
La Marzocco
Linea PB

GRINDER
Nuova Simonelli
Mythos One

OPENING HOURS
Tue–Thu
10am–10pm
Fri–Sat
10am–11pm

 BEANS AVAILABLE INSTORE

 WIFI

 CYCLE FRIENDLY

 OUTDOOR SEATING

 DISABLED ACCESS

 BRING YOUR OWN CUP

 DOG FRIENDLY

07999 994641

 f @bayleysbromsgrove 🐦 @bayleysofbrom 📷 @bayleys_of_bromsgrove

118 WAYLAND'S YARD – WORCESTER

6 Foregate Street, Worcester, WR1 1DB

Wayland's Yard's flagship venue is a coffee shop striving to deliver life's essentials of "proper coffee" and "proper food" in style.

It achieves its aim, and then some, by slinging own-roasted coffee (alongside a line-up of guest beans) and dishing out a no-nonsense take on brunch. Never have crumpets taken on so many wonderful incarnations as they do at Wayland's. Who says you can't put fried cornflake-chicken and crispy bacon on top of a fluffy, egg-dipped crumpet? It's only bettered by a post-crumpet petting of an equally fluffy delight: resident spaniel Kobe who likes to make new two- and four-legged friends.

 INSIDER'S TIP: INDULGE YOUR INNER CHILD ON THE SWING SEATS IN THE SECRET GARDEN

During lockdown, the team embarked on some major innovations. They took on an abandoned roastery unit in Bristol to fulfil their dream of roasting their own coffee, and brought all the baking in-house – including the crafting of their legendary sticky cinnamon buns. House-roasted Odd Kin coffee is now served as standard in the line-up of espresso and pourover drinks, and is best combined with one of the homemade carby treats.

ESTABLISHED
2016

KEY ROASTER
Odd Kin
Coffee Roasters

BREWING METHOD
Espresso, V60,
AeroPress

MACHINE
Victoria Arduino
Eagle One

GRINDER
Mahlkonig E80,
Mahlkonig EK43,
Mahlkonig E65S
GbW

OPENING HOURS
Mon-Fri
7am-6pm
Sat
8am-6pm
Sun
8am-5pm

Gluten FREE

BEANS AVAILABLE IN STORE

WIFI

OUTDOOR SEATING

DISABLED ACCESS

BRING YOUR OWN CUP

DOG FRIENDLY

---

www.waylandsyard.com

 @waylandsyard @waylandsyard @waylandsyard

119 ABBEY ROAD COFFEE

11 Abbey Road, Great Malvern, Worcestershire, WR14 3ES

Abbey Road Coffee is a family-run speciality coffee shop that enjoys a lovely location at the foot of the Malvern Hills. The recently refurbished venue is a popular spot with coffee lovers and dog owners alike (check out its Instagram for pics of good-boy guests) thanks to its spacious indoor and outdoor seating and pukka brews.

The house coffee is a bespoke blend, care of Worcester's Method Coffee Roasters, which is joined by a rotating line-up of guest single-origin options. In addition to the classic espresso drinks, visitors can revel in seasonal coffees via V60 and batch brew.

 OPT FOR OAT MILK IN YOUR DRINK AND GET A CHEEKY DISCOUNT

The plant-based leaning of the cafe goes somewhat under the radar as there's no preaching going on: the homemade cakes are incredible and, as it happens, also vegan. Regulars featuring within the groaning cake cabinet include a coconut and chocolate Bounty slice, lightly spiced carrot cake, flaky almond croissants, salted caramel brownies, and soft and chewy filled snickerdoodle cookie-sandwiches. Veganism never tasted so sweet.

ESTABLISHED
2015

KEY ROASTER
Method Coffee Roasters

BREWING METHOD
Espresso, V60, Moccamaster

MACHINE
La Marzocco Linea PB

GRINDER
Mahlkonig E65S x 2, Mahlkonig K30, Nuova Simonelli Mythos

OPENING HOURS
Mon-Sat
8.30am-4.30pm
Sun
9am-4pm

 Gluten FREE

 BEANS AVAILABLE INSTORE

 WIFI

 CYCLE FRIENDLY

 OUTDOOR SEATING

 BRING YOUR OWN Cup

 DOG FRIENDLY

www.abbeyroadcoffee.co.uk   07947 209886

f @abbeyroadcoffee   @abbeyroadcoffee

Roasteries

The Midlands

120 SEVEN DISTRICTS COFFEE

Farmers Arms, Market Rasen Road, Lincoln, Lincolnshire, LN2 3RD

There are hundreds of stories behind every cup of coffee – from the farmer's walk to work on the day of picking, to the home brewer hastily grinding beans after a missed wake-up alarm – and this roastery was established to tell the tales behind the beans.

'We believe the love of coffee is not just about enjoying a simple beverage. At its heart it's about the communities built when stories are shared between friends, old and new, over a delicious coffee,' say founders Ben Southall and Ellis Purvis.

ESTABLISHED
2019

ROASTER MAKE & SIZE
Custom built roasters x 2 12kg

'A COFFEE SUBSCRIPTION WHICH DELIVERS FRESHLY ROASTED COFFEE AND A FREE BOOK'

Eight unique roasts (seven single origins and a blend) provide the springboard for conversation at Seven Districts, and are directly sourced from Peru, Ethiopia, Nicaragua, Rwanda, Colombia and Brazil. The roasting magic happens at a pub-turned-roastery, where the team have installed two custom-made roasters and a takeaway hatch. There's also a sister coffee shop in Nettleham.

Storytelling is such an important part of the Seven Districts ethos that Ben and Ellis have also launched the Seven Districts Society – a coffee subscription which delivers a three-monthly bundle of freshly roasted coffee and includes a free book.

---

www.sevendistrictscoffee.com   01673 885901

f *@sevendistrictscoffee*   🐦 *@sevendcoffee*   📷 *@sevendistrictscoffee*

121 CARTWHEEL COFFEE ROASTERS

Unit S1, Roden House, Roden Street, Nottingham, NG3 1JH

Every bag of Cartwheel coffee pays tribute to the many farmers, importers, roasters, baristas and customers associated with the Nottingham roastery.

Owner Alex Bitsios-Esposito says: *'It's people who make everything we do at Cartwheel achievable and meaningful. Without them we wouldn't exist. So, with every bag of coffee, we attempt in some small way to honour and recognise the many people who make it all possible.'*

ESTABLISHED
2015

ROASTER MAKE & SIZE
Probat P12 12kg

OPEN BY APPOINTMENT

COFFEE COURSES

BEANS AVAILABLE

'IT'S PEOPLE WHO MAKE EVERYTHING WE DO AT CARTWHEEL ACHIEVABLE AND MEANINGFUL'

The team are dedicated to looking after the planet and minimising environmental impact, and recently introduced new vacuum-packed, nitrogen-flushed coffee bags.

'These are 100 per cent recyclable, and the tasting card attached to each one is made entirely from recycled coffee cups,' adds Alex.

The flourishing roastery is committed to tracking down the best coffees in the world and preserving their unique flavours through its roasting process. The team recently opened a second cafe in the heart of Beeston (joining the city-centre original), and have also launched a new website and started offering tailored coffee-subscriptions.

www.cartwheelcoffee.com   01159 589269
f @cartwheelcoffee   🅞 @cartwheelcoffee

122 STEWARTS OF TRENT BRIDGE

Unit 31, Avenue C, Sneinton Market, Nottingham, NG1 1DW

In 1984, Nottingham-based coffee visionary Stewart Falconer began hand-roasting coffee that matched the exceptional quality he'd experienced on his travels overseas. Almost 40 years on, the roastery he established and the ethos behind it are stronger than ever.

Stewarts of Trent Bridge operates from Sneinton Market, a converted fruit and veg market in Nottingham's creative hub. The Stewarts team is made up of ethically minded coffee addicts who enjoy choosing coffee they love to drink themselves – and sharing it with their customers.

'A STATE-OF-THE-ART FILTRATION SYSTEM MINIMISES ROASTERY FUMES'

The seasonally shifting roster includes a Colombian coffee bought direct from the farm and other high-scoring beans from Honduras, Brazil and Papua New Guinea. Find the full line-up online or sample the Sunset Espresso and Road Trip blends at indie cafes across Nottingham.

The business recently made a big investment in lowering its carbon footprint by installing a state-of-the-art filtration system that minimises roastery fumes. See it for yourself on a roastery tour – available by appointment.

ESTABLISHED
1984

ROASTER MAKE & SIZE
Toper 20kg
Ikawa

CAFE ONSITE

OPEN BY APPOINTMENT

COFFEE COURSES

BEANS AVAILABLE

www.stewartscoffees.co.uk   01158 389351
f @stewartscoffees @stewartscoffeesuk

123 OUTPOST COFFEE ROASTERS

32 Salisbury Square, Nottingham, Nottinghamshire, NG7 2AB

There's a three-pronged approach at this Nottingham roastery that ensures every single cup crafted from Outpost beans is of the highest quality.

The first focus is on sourcing: the team take great care to ensure they only work with farmers who are committed to growing standout coffees and paid fairly for their hard work. The roastery's mainly single-origin offering means they source from a vast range of countries – from Burundi and Ethiopia to Colombia and India.

'THEY ONLY WORK WITH FARMERS WHO ARE COMMITTED TO GROWING STANDOUT COFFEES'

Next on the Outpost agenda is roasting. The gang recently upgraded their Petrocini roaster to a chunkier 20kg model, enabling them to increase their batch size to meet growing demand from cafe and consumer customers. They've also updated the tech used to tailor the roast so they can coax a kaleidoscope of flavours from the precious greens.

The final aim is training. To get the very best out of every cup, Outpost works with all of its industry partners to ensure the baristas' skills are level with the quality of the coffee. Amateur espresso slingers can polish up their act too: masterclasses for home brewers are available to book online.

ESTABLISHED
2014

ROASTER MAKE & SIZE
Petrocini TT 20
20kg

COFFEE
COURSES

BEANS
AVAILABLE

ONLINE

---

www.outpost.coffee   **01158 374320**

f @outpostcoffee   ⦿ @outpostcoffeeroasters

124 COURTYARD COFFEE ROASTERS

14d High Street, Eccleshall, Staffordshire, ST21 6BZ

Courtyard Coffee has been in the roasting game since the early 1980s. While its original roaster has been traded in for a newer model (a cherry-red Diedrich 2.5kg Infra Red Drum machine), the company ethos remains the same: to work exclusively with ethical importers and roast the best beans in small batches.

Regardless of their country of origin, founder David Wiggins allows the coffee to fully develop during roasting, where he opts for a sweet and toasty medium–city roast. Beans are sourced from Africa, India, Indonesia, Central America and South America, resulting in a Courtyard collection of around 20 single–origin arabicas and high–quality blends.

ESTABLISHED
2015

ROASTER MAKE & SIZE
Diedrich 2.5kg

OPEN
BY APPOINTMENT

COFFEE
COURSES

BEANS
AVAILABLE

'FOUNDER DAVID WIGGINS OPTS FOR A SWEET AND TOASTY MEDIUM–CITY ROAST'

David recently expanded Courtyard's range of decaffeinated beans and there are now at least three options at any time, all of which are water processed. Beans are available online and on–site, while roastery tours are available by appointment.

www.courtyardcoffeeroasters.co.uk   **01785 851024**
f @courtyardcoffeeroasters

125 HASBEAN

Unit 16, Ladford Covert, Ladfordfields Industrial Estate, Stafford, Staffordshire, ST18 9QL

E stablished in 2002, before most people in the UK had even heard of a flat white, this Staffordshire roastery has been at the forefront of the speciality coffee scene for almost two decades.

Today, Hasbean is a leader in the industry, curating one of the most comprehensive collections of speciality-grade beans in Europe. Roasting daily on six top-of-the-range machines, the skilled team offer up to 30 different roasts at any one time – all of which can be obtained via the online shop.

'CURATING ONE OF THE MOST COMPREHENSIVE COLLECTIONS IN EUROPE'

The line-up features hero blends such as Jailbreak (a long-term fave featuring notes of milk chocolate, white sugar, caramel and almond), alongside limited-edition blends and globetrotting single origins. The Hasbean team travel the world in search of the finest beans and select lots for their unique flavours and sustainable credentials.

The best way to sample the spectrum is via the Hasbean subscription, which offers a huge range of personalised options, so customers can find the perfect beans for their coffee-drinking habits. The team even put together a weekly In My Mug videocast to add another dimension to coffee drinkers' Hasbean experience.

ESTABLISHED
2002

ROASTER MAKE & SIZE
Probat G60
60kg
Probat L25 25kg
Probat P12 12kg
Ambex YM-H2
2kg
Vintage Probat
Vintage
Pinhalense

www.hasbean.co.uk   07507 411924
f @hasbeancoffee   🐦 @hasbean   📷 @hasbean

126 HUNDRED HOUSE COFFEE

Baucott Barn, Baucott, Craven Arms, Shropshire, SY7 9HJ

The team at this roastery craft coffee for speciality enthusiasts, and the collection of Hundred House beans – sourced from sustainable growers – gives coffee lovers the chance to experience rare single origins and unique blends.

Beans arrive at the roastery from a wide range of countries including Kenya, Burundi, Rwanda, Tanzania, Nicaragua and Peru, while roasting takes place in rural Shropshire on a Diedrich IR-12 roaster (which can be seen in action on a roastery tour – by appointment).

ESTABLISHED
2016

ROASTER MAKE & SIZE
Diedrich
IR-12 12kg

OPEN
BY APPOINTMENT

BEANS
AVAILABLE
ONLINE

'A CURATED CURIOSITY COLLECTION OF THE MOST OFF-THE-WALL COFFEES'

Everything about this roastery is unconventional so naturally the house blends have playful names: Bon Bon (a sweet, jammy seasonal espresso), CoCo (a chocolatey espresso), Nom Nom (an espresso with double the flavour and half the caffeine) and Vida (an organic espresso).

In 2020, Hundred House launched its Freak & Unique collection: a *'curated curiosity collection of the most off-the-wall coffees'* the team could find, to highlight the outstanding and unusual. A percentage of their sale price goes towards the roastery's Art + Industry Programme which supports independent creatives.

---

www.hundredhousecoffee.com   01584 841206

f @hundredhousecoffee   🐦 @hundredhouseco   📷 @hundredhousecoffee

127 QUARTER HORSE COFFEE

88-90 Bristol Street, Birmingham, West Midlands, B5 7AH

Founded in 2012, Quarter Horse Coffee was the first combined cafe and roastery in Birmingham. It's still one of the only coffee roasteries in the country to offer ringside tables with full view of the roasting action.

Founder and Q grader Nathan Retzer prepares a constantly changing range of high-quality beans which are carefully selected for their seasonality, ethical credentials and exceptional flavour. They're test-roasted in small batches, then cupped and graded, before the team's favourites make their way onto the shelves of the on-site coffee shop, appear in the online store, and are delivered to indie cafes across the UK.

'RINGSIDE TABLES WITH FULL VIEW OF THE ROASTING ACTION'

Where possible, the team import directly from coffee farmers, and prioritise lasting relationships, positive development and ethical practices at origin. Beans are imported from North, South and Central America, East Africa, the Middle East and Asia.

New to Quarter Horse? The Roaster's Selection retail pack with its four expertly chosen seasonal coffees is the perfect introduction.

ESTABLISHED
2012

ROASTER MAKE & SIZE
Giesen W15A
15kg

CAFE ONSITE

OPEN BY APPOINTMENT

COFFEE COURSES

BEANS AVAILABLE
ONLINE ONSITE

---

www.quarterhorsecoffee.com   01214 489660
f @quarterhorsecoffee   🐦 @qtrhorsecoffee   📷 @quarterhorsecoffee

More good COFFEE SHOPS

Further places to drink exceptional coffee

128 BALTZERSEN'S

22 Oxford Street, Harrogate,
North Yorkshire, HG1 1PU
www.baltzersens.co.uk

129 BEAN AND LEAF COFFEE HOUSE

67 Hertford Street, Coventry, CV1 1LB
www.beanandleafcoffeehouse.co.uk

130 BEDFORD ST COFFEE

27 Bedford Street, Middlesbrough,
North Yorkshire, TS1 2LL
www.rountoncoffee.co.uk

131 BLOOMFIELD SQUARE

28–30 Gay Lane, Otley, Leeds,
West Yorkshire, LS21 1BR

132 BREW & BITE – GOSFORTH

27 Ashburton Road, Gosforth,
Newcastle upon Tyne, NE3 4XN
www.brewandbitecoffee.co.uk

133 CARTWHEEL COFFEE – BEESTON

1a Stoney Street, Beeston,
Nottingham, NG9 2LA
www.cartwheelcoffee.com

134 CARTWHEEL COFFEE – NOTTINGHAM

16 Low Pavement, Nottingham, NG1 7DL
www.cartwheelcoffee.com

135 COFFI

8 Pilgrim Street, Liverpool, L1 9HB
www.coffiliverpool.com

136 DR BREWS COFFEE

3 Grosvenor Terrace, Bowness-
on-Windermere, Windermere,
Cumbria, LA23 3BS

137 DREAMBAKES

3 Priory House, Priory Walk, Doncaster,
South Yorkshire, DN1 1TS
www.dreambakes.co.uk

138 ESPRESSO CORNER

11 Kirkgate, Huddersfield,
West Yorkshire, HD1 1QS

139 EXCHANGE COFFEE COMPANY – BLACKBURN MARKET

Stall F9/1, Blackburn Market,
Ainsworth Street, Blackburn,
Lancashire, BB1 5AF
www.exchangecoffee.co.uk

140 EXCHANGE COFFEE COMPANY – CLITHEROE

24 Wellgate, Clitheroe,
Lancashire, BB7 2DP
www.exchangecoffee.co.uk

141 EXCHANGE COFFEE COMPANY – SKIPTON

10 Gargrave Road, Skipton,
North Yorkshire, BD23 1PJ
www.exchangecoffee.co.uk

142 EZRA & GIL

20 Hilton Street, Northern Quarter,
Manchester, M1 1FR
www.ezraandgil.com

143 FEDERAL CAFE & BAR – DEANSGATE

194 Deansgate, Manchester, M3 3ND
www.federalcafe.co.uk

144 FEDERAL CAFE & BAR – NICHOLAS CROFT

9 Nicholas Croft, Northern Quarter,
Manchester, M4 1EY
www.federalcafe.co.uk

145 FLAT WHITE KITCHEN

40 Saddler Street, Durham, DH1 3NU
www.flatwhitekitchen.com

146 FOUNDATION COFFEE HOUSE – NQ

Sevendale House, Lever Street,
Manchester, M1 1JB
www.foundationcoffeehouse.co.uk

147 FOUNDATION COFFEE HOUSE – WHITWORTH

48–50 Whitworth Street,
Manchester, M1 6LS
www.foundationcoffeehouse.co.uk

148 GRINDSMITH COFFEE POD

15 Pollard Street East,
Manchester, M40 7QX
www.grindsmith.com

149 HOXTON NORTH

1a Royal Parade, Harrogate,
North Yorkshire, HG1 2SZ
www.hoxtonnorth.com

150 JAUNTY GOAT – BAKERY

50a Bridge Street, Chester,
Cheshire, CH1 1NQ
www.jauntygoat.co.uk

151 JOE'SPRESSO

404 South Road, Walkley, Sheffield,
South Yorkshire, S6 3TF
www.joespresso.co.uk

152 LA BOTTEGA MILANESE

2 Bond Court, Leeds,
West Yorkshire, LS1 2JZ
www.labottegamilanese.co.uk

153 LANEWAY & CO

17-19 High Bridge, Newcastle
upon Tyne, NE1 1EW

154 LONGFORD CAFE

Longford Park, Manchester, M32 8DA

155 MADAME WAFFLE

285 High Street, Lincoln, LN2 1AL
www.madamewaffle.co.uk

156 MARMADUKES CAFE DELI

22 Norfolk Row, Sheffield,
South Yorkshire, S1 2PA
www.marmadukes.co

157 METHOD COFFEE ROASTERS

Arch 50/51, Cherry Tree Walk,
Worcester, WR1 3BH
www.methodroastery.com

158 MINI BEANS COFFEE

Crewe Market Hall, Earle Street, Crewe,
Cheshire, CW1 2BL
www.minibeanscoffee.com

159 NO35 HARROGATE

35 Cheltenham Crescent, Harrogate,
North Yorkshire, HG1 1DH
www.no35harrogate.coffee

160 NORTH STAR COFFEE

Unit 32, Leeds Dock, The Boulevard,
Leeds, West Yorkshire, LS10 1PZ
www.northstarroast.com

161 NORTHERN EDGE COFFEE

7 Silver Street, Berwick-upon-Tweed,
Northumberland, TD15 1HU

www.northernedgecoffee.co.uk

162 NUMBER THIRTEEN COFFEE HOUSE & CAKERY

13 Castlegate, Knaresborough,
North Yorkshire, HG5 8AR
www.thirteencastlegate.com

163 OBSCURE COFFEE

66 Lower Bridge Street, Chester,
Cheshire, CH1 1RU

164 OLD GEORGE – HERITAGE

Wellington Mills, 70 Plover Road,
Huddersfield, West Yorkshire, HD3 3HR
www.old-george.co.uk

165 OLD GEORGE – TOWN HALL

Town Hall, Church Street, Barnsley,
South Yorkshire, S70 2TA
www.old-george.co.uk

166 PANNA

35 Watergate Street, Chester,
Cheshire, CH1 2LB

167 PILGRIM'S COFFEE HOUSE

Marygate, The Holy Island of Lindisfarne,
Northumberland, TD15 2SJ
www.pilgrimscoffee.com

168 ROOST COFFEE – ESPRESSO BAR

Unit 6, Talbot Yard, Yorkersgate, Malton,
North Yorkshire, YO17 7FT
www.roostcoffee.co.uk

169 STEAM YARD

Unit 1-2, Aberdeen Court,
97 Division Street, Sheffield,
South Yorkshire, S1 4GE
www.steamyard.co.uk

170 TAKK – UNIVERSITY GREEN

138 Oxford Road, Manchester, M13 9GP
www.takkmcr.com

171 TAKK ESPRESSO BAR

Unit 1, Hatch, Oxford Road,
Manchester, M1 7ED
www.takkmcr.com

172 TAMPER

149 Arundel Street, Sheffield,
South Yorkshire, S1 2NU
www.tampercoffee.co.uk

173 THE BIRDS NEST CAFE

Claremont Street, Shrewsbury,
Shropshire, SY1 1QG
www.thebirdsnestcafe.co.uk

174 THE BOOKSHOP

32 Aubrey Street, Hereford, HR4 0BU
www.aruleoftum.com

175 THE BREW SOCIETY

26 Aire Street, Leeds,
West Yorkshire, LS1 4HT
www.brewsociety.co.uk

176 THE FLOWER CUP

61 Watergate Row South,
Chester, CH1 2LE
www.flowercup.co.uk

177 THE MOON & SIXPENCE COFFEEHOUSE

29 Main Street, Cockermouth,
Cumbria, CA13 9LE

178 THE SNUG COFFEE HOUSE

67a Market Street, Atherton,
Greater Manchester, M46 0DA

179 TROVE

5 Murray Street, Ancoats,
Manchester, M4 6HS
www.trovefoods.co.uk

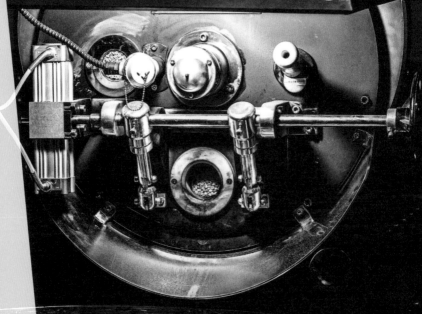

More good
ROASTERIES
Additional beans for your home hopper

180 BLOSSOM COFFEE ROASTERS

The Old Bank Residency, Hanover Street,
Noma, Manchester, M4 4AH
www.blossomcoffee.co.uk

181 BUXTON COFFEE ROASTERS

Unit 20b Kiln Lane, Harpur Hill
Business Park, Buxton,
Peak District, SK17 9JL
www.buxtoncoffeeroasters.co.uk

182 CASA ESPRESSO

Unit 5, Briar Rhydding House, Otley Road,
Shipley, West Yorkshire, BD17 7JW
www.casaespresso.co.uk

183 CLO COFFEE

41 Main Street, Garforth, Leeds,
West Yorkshire, LS25 1DS
www.clocoffee.com

184 EXCHANGE COFFEE COMPANY

24 Wellgate, Clitheroe,
Lancashire, BB7 2DP
www.exchangecoffee.co.uk

185 GRINDSMITH COFFEE ROASTERS

Unit 6, Varley Business Centre,
Manchester, M40 8EL
www.grindsmith.com

186 HEART AND GRAFT COFFEE ROASTERY

30 Holyoak Street, Manchester, M40 1HB
www.heartandgraft.co.uk

187 JOLLY BEAN ROASTERY

15 Victoria Road, Saltaire,
West Yorkshire, BD18 3LQ
www.jollybeanroastery.co.uk

188 MANCOCO

Arch 84, Hewitt Street,
Manchester, M15 4GB
www.mancoco.co.uk

189 MAUDE COFFEE ROASTERS

82-83 Railway Street, Leeds,
West Yorkshire, LS9 8HB
www.maudecoffee.co.uk

190 METHOD COFFEE ROASTERS

Arches 50-51, Cherry Tree Walk,
Worcester, WR1 3BH
www.methodroastery.com

191 MONSOON ESTATES COFFEE COMPANY

Unit 2, Alscot Park, Atherstone on Stour,
Warwickshire, CV37 8BL
www.monsoonestatescoffee.co.uk

192 MR DUFFINS COFFEE

49 Main Street, Staveley, Kendal,
Cumbria, LA8 9LN
www.mrduffinscoffee.com

193 NORTH STAR COFFEE ROASTERS

Unit 10, 280 Tong Road, Leeds,
West Yorkshire, LS12 3BG
www.northstarroast.com

194 NORTHERN EDGE COFFEE

7 Silver Street, Berwick-upon-Tweed,
Northumberland, TD15 1HU
www.northernedgecoffee.co.uk

195 PENNINGTONS TEA AND COFFEE

Unit 12, Kendal Business Park,
Appleby Road, Kendal, Cumbria, LA9 6EW
www.penningtonscoffee.co.uk

196 POCOESPRESSO

29 The Gables, Cottam, Preston,
Lancashire, PR4 0LB
www.pocoespresso.com

197 RED BANK COFFEE ROASTERS

Units 12-13, Boundary Bank, Kendal,
Cumbria, LA9 5RR
www.redbankcoffee.com

198 ROBERTS & CO.

Cedar Farm, Back Lane, Mawdesley,
Ormskirk, Lancashire, L40 3SY
www.e-coffee.co.uk

199 ROUNTON COFFEE ROASTERS

East Rounton, Northallerton,
North Yorkshire, DL6 2LG
www.rountoncoffee.co.uk

MEET OUR COMMITTEE

The *North, Midlands and North Wales Independent Coffee Guide* committee is made up of a small band of leading coffee experts from across the region who have worked with Salt Media and the coffee community to oversee the creation of this year's guide

Dave Olejnik

Having always sought out great coffee shops, it was during Dave's time living in Seattle (where he worked as a touring guitar tech) that he was inspired to fully divert his energy into coffee. He returned to the UK and worked for Coffee Community, travelling the world as a trainer and consultant before launching Laynes Espresso in Leeds in 2011.

Dave opened his second venue, Dot the Lions, at Leeds Arts University in 2019. Later that year he also launched Sarto, a restaurant built around a winning menu of handmade pasta, interesting wines and, of course, great coffee.

Matthew Wade

Fine-art graduate Matthew trained as a barista and roaster in New Zealand. He brought his coffee experience with him when he returned to London which led to him playing a leading role in the burgeoning UK coffee scene of the early noughties.

Matthew became one of the UK's first Q graders and won several awards for his coffees when he was head roaster at Union Hand-Roasted and Bullet Coffee.

In 2011 he moved to the Middle East and was instrumental in developing its third-wave coffee movement, as well as co-founding Dubai's Nightjar Coffee. On his return to the UK in 2016, Matthew set up Hundred House Coffee, a multi-award-winning roastery in Shropshire.

Hannah Davies

Paul Meikle-Janney

Hannah's long career in the coffee industry saw her develop from a barista in Liverpool to a training manager and authorised SCA trainer for a national coffee company. Her current role as relationship manager with The Barista League allows her to fulfil her commitment to the coffee community in the UK and across Europe.

Since 2014, Hannah has worked with the Manchester coffee scene to create Manchester Coffee Festival, an event dedicated to showcasing the speciality coffee industry of the North and beyond.

Paul is a founder of Dark Woods Coffee, the multi-award-winning rural roastery on the outskirts of Huddersfield.

In 1999, Paul started Coffee Community, an international training and consultancy agency for the speciality industry. He's co-written both the City & Guilds and SCA barista qualifications and has been involved in the World Barista Championships and UK Barista Championships since their inception. He was also head judge at the World Latte Art and World Coffee in Good Spirits championships for four years.

When he's not fulfilling SCA Education Committee duties, Paul tends his ever-growing house and jazz record collection.

Ian Steel

When, in 2005, Ian and wife Sue acquired Lancaster coffee and tea merchants Atkinsons, their career change was partly inspired by the desire to find financial security in the retail and hospitality sector.

'We spent years building the brand and enjoying the people we met through coffee,' says Ian, *'but no-one could've seen the juggernaut marked Covid heading straight towards us. Suddenly hospitality was shut and retail went online.*

'Like many, we became a fully digital company overnight and the untapped potential of our online audience awoke like a sleeping giant.'

Like all independent businesses, the Atkinsons team are emerging from the storm, looking around at the new landscape and wondering: *what next?*

'We're still doing far more online than ever. New markets have emerged, such as the new homeworkers, and customers are returning to our cafes in droves.'

Index

	Entry no
200 Degrees	45

a

Abbey Road Coffee	119
Albie's Coffee	96
Ancoats Coffee Co.	
– *111 Piccadilly*	50
– *roastery*	60
– *Royal Mills*	47
Arcade Coffee & Food	90
Archive	82
Atkinsons	
– *Shop and Roastery*	30
– *The Castle*	9
– *The Hall*	10
– *The Mackie Mayor*	46
– *The Music Room*	11

b

Baltzersen's	128
Bank Coffeehouse, The	113
Baristocracy Coffee	6
Bayley's of Bromsgrove	117
Bean & Bud	70
Bean & Cole	57
Bean and Leaf Coffee House	129
Bean Loved	73
Bean There Coffee Shop	25
Bedford St Coffee	130
Birds Nest Cafe, The	173

	Entry no
Blend Coffee House	
– *East West*	109
– *Sneinton Market*	111
Bloc	92
Bloomfield Square	131
Blossom Coffee Roasters	180
Bold Street Coffee	23
Bookshop, The	174
Bowery	79
Brew & Bite	
– *Gosforth*	132
– *Heaton*	3
Brew Society, The	175
Brew Twenty Three	116
Buxton Coffee Roasters	181

c

Caffé & Co.	18
Caffe Figo	107
Cartwheel Coffee	
– *Beeston*	133
– *Nottingham*	134
Cartwheel Coffee Roasters	121
Carvetii Coffee Roasters	27
Casa Espresso	182
Cedarwood Coffee Company	15
Claypath Deli	4
CLO Coffee	183
Clubhouse Coffee & Cycles, The	75
Coffee on the Crescent	80
Coffeevolution	89

Entry no

c

COFFI	135
Comida [food]	8
Courtyard Coffee Roasters	124
Crosby Coffee	
- *Lark Lane*	24
- *Oxford Road*	19
Crosby Coffee Roasters	31
Curious Coffee Company, The	
- *Easingwold*	69
- *Haxby*	68

d-e

Dark Woods Coffee	101
Django Coffee Co.	33
Dot the Lions	81
Dr Brews Coffee	136
Dreambakes	137
Echelon Coffee Roasters	100
Espresso Corner	138
Exchange Coffee Company	184
- *Blackburn Market*	139
- *Clitheroe*	140
- *Skipton*	141
Ezra & Gil	142

f-g

Federal Cafe & Bar	
- *Deansgate*	143
- *Nicholas Croft*	144
Fig + Sparrow	48
Fika Coffee Roasters	7

Entry no

Fika North	78
Flat White Kitchen	145
Flower Cup, The	176
Forge Coffee Roasters	103
Foundation Coffee House	
- *NQ*	146
- *Whitworth*	147
Frank Street Coffee House	13
Frazer's Coffee Roasters	102
Ginger & Co.	106
Greenhood Coffee	112
Grind & Tamp	41
Grindsmith Coffee Pod	148
Grindsmith Coffee Roasters	
- *cafe*	43
- *roastery*	185

h-j

Hampton & Vouis	44
Hasbean	125
Hatch Luncheonette	5
Haus	36
Heart and Graft Coffee Roasters	186
Heartland Coffee Roasters	39
Heather & Batch Coffee House	108
Hoxton North	149
Hundred House Coffee	126
Jaunty Goat	63
Jaunty Goat Coffee	
- *Bakery*	150
- *Bridge Street*	58
- *Northgate Street*	56
Joe'spresso	151
Jolly Bean Roastery	187
Journey Social Kitchen	12

k-l

Kapow Coffee	84
Kickback Coffee	61
Kigali	110
Kirkby Lonsdale Coffee Roasters	29
Koda	65
KRA:FT Koffee	93
La Bottega Milanese	152
Laneway & Co	153
Lay of the Land	72
Laynes Espresso	85
Liar Liar	105
Little Yellow Pig	54
Longford Cafe	154

m-n

Madame Waffle	155
ManCoCo	188
Marmadukes Cafe Deli	156
Maude Coffee Roasters	189
Method Coffee Roasters	
– *cafe*	157
– *roastery*	190
Mini Beans Coffee	158
Monsoon Estates Coffee Company	191
Moon & Sixpence Coffeehouse, The	177
Mow's Coffee	97
Mr Duffins Coffee	192
Neighbourhood Coffee	32
No35 Harrogate	159
NØRTH Kitchen + Bar	104
North Star Coffee	160

North Star Coffee Roasters	193
Northern Edge Coffee	
– *cafe*	161
– *roastery*	194
Number Thirteen Coffee House & Cakery	162

o-p

Obscure Coffee	163
Off the Ground	64
Old George	
– *Heritage*	164
– *Town Hall*	165
Old George Coffee House	94
One Percent Forest	26
Out of the Woods	
– *Granary Wharf*	86
– *Water Lane*	87
Outpost Coffee Roasters	123
Panna	166
Penningtons Tea and Coffee	195
Pilgrim's Coffee House	167
Poblado Coffi	40
pocoespresso	196
Propeller Coffee	51
Providero	
– *Llandudno*	34
– *Llandudno Junction*	35
PureKnead	1

q-r

Quarter Horse Coffee	
– *cafe*	115
– *roastery*	127

q-r

Red Bank Coffee Roasters	197
Rinaldo's Speciality Coffee & Fine Tea	28
Rise.	14
Riverbanc	37
Roberts & Co.	198
Roost Coffee – Espresso Bar	168
Roost Coffee & Roastery	98
Root Coffee	22
Rounton Coffee Roasters	199
Rustic Cup	2

s

Salford Roasters	59
Sam's Coffee at Gales	38
Sea Shanty, The	21
Seven Districts Coffee	120
SHORT + STOUT	55
Siphon Espresso & Brew Bar	16
Snug Coffee House, The	178
Squeeze Cafe & Deli	88
Stage Espresso & Brew Bar	83
Starling Independent Bar Cafe Kitchen	71
Steam Yard	169
Steep & Filter	74
Stewarts of Trent Bridge	122
SUP	20

t-y

Takk Coffee House and Brunch Kitchen	49
Takk Espresso Bar	171
Takk – University Green	170
Tambourine Coffee	77
Tamper	172
Toast House	76
TROVE	179
Two Brothers	
– roastery	62
– Altrincham	52
– St Helens	17
– Warrington	53
Two Gingers Coffee	67
Wayland's Yard	
– Birmingham	114
– Worcester	118
Weaver and Wilde	42
Whaletown Coffee Company, The	95
Wired Coffee and Cake	91
Yay Coffee!	66
York Emporium	99

NOTES

Somewhere to keep a record of
exceptional beans and brews you've
discovered on your coffee adventures

NOTES

Somewhere to keep a record of
exceptional beans and brews you've
discovered on your coffee adventures

NOTES

Somewhere to keep a record of
exceptional beans and brews you've
discovered on your coffee adventures

FOR BREW FREAKS, BEAN GEEKS

AND THE SIMPLY CURIOUS ...